HAUNTINGLY
GOOD SPIRITS

HAUNTINGLY
GOOD SPIRITS

NEW ORLEANS COCKTAILS TO DIE FOR

SHARON KEATING CHRISTI KEATING SUMICH

castle

NEW ORLEANS IS
THE ONLY CITY THAT
I'VE BEEN IN THAT
IF YOU LISTEN
THE SIDEWALKS
WILL SPEAK TO YOU.

JOHN T. SCOTT
SCULPTOR, PAINTER, PRINTMAKER, COLLAGIST,
AND NEW ORLEANS'S SON

CONTENTS

INTRODUCTION
CHEERS TO THE CITY OF THE DEAD

NEW ORLEANS IS AN ENIGMA. It is known as the city that care forgot due to its *joie de vivre* ("joy of living") and *laissez les bons temps rouler* ("let the good times roll") attitude. You may have also heard the city called Necropolis due to the high number of deaths following the late-eighteenth-century yellow fever epidemic. But it's also known as the City of the Dead, a moniker referring to the above-ground cemeteries that are so prevalent in the city's landscape and culture.

New Orleans primarily buries her dead above ground in tombs and crypts because the city is below sea level. Flooding can dislodge coffins buried below and cause them to rise to the surface, which can be unsettling even for the biggest fan of spooky stuff. There is debate about whether high water tables require above-ground burial, as flooding can render even vaults buoyant, causing them to drift away with their caskets. Nevertheless, following the tradition observed in France and Spain, above-ground tombs became the logical, though not fail-safe, choice for New Orleans cemeteries.

Within the primary City of the Dead are smaller Cities of the Dead, a term also used for New Orleans's famous cemeteries. They earned this nickname because they resemble small villages complete with named and mapped streets. Large, ornate tombs and crypts are lined up on either side of the tree-lined streets. These above-ground tombs that pepper the city and surrounding areas ensure that the dead mingle with the living daily. No matter where you live, in or around the city, you pass these cemeteries on a regular basis. They are so common that they have become part of the landscape and blend into their surroundings almost seamlessly.

Cocktails share a similar cultural importance in New Orleans, the birthplace of many colorful cocktails. Drinking in general is more than a means to an end in

New Orleans culture; it's a way of celebrating life—an Olympic-level pastime for the city's residents. In fact, when preparing for hurricanes, many of us have been guilty of heading straight to the liquor aisle as our first stop for provisions. So, naturally, cocktails are serious business here. And the seriousness extends beyond financial considerations (with tourism and the abundance of bars and restaurants) into a cultlike devotion to creating a classic cocktail with specific ingredients and precise preparation methods.

The acts of crafting and consuming cocktails are as ritualized as jazz funerals and just as full of shared social connections. New Orleans is a place where walking down the street with a to-go cup of spirits is considered normal, especially if your destination is a Mardi Gras parade. From mimosas at a Sunday brunch with family to an evening cocktail on the front porch with neighbors, New Orleanians enjoy sharing good times and good cocktails with good friends.

But why would you choose a cocktail bearing a name associated with death for your celebratory imbibing? Cocktails with creepy names, whether originating in New Orleans or simply aligning well with its ambience, epitomize the paradox of enjoying life in a city that has a thriving culture of death. The cocktails we feature are a lens through which we can view New Orleans's unique connection with death, burial customs, and funeral practices as ironically life-affirming, not always definitive, and generally a cause for celebration. We weave into our cocktails the city's paranormal energy, touching on ghosts, Voodoo, and vampires. So, if you prefer your cocktails with a dash of bitters and a garnish of atmosphere, read on!

BREW YOUR POTIONS
HOW TO USE THIS BOOK

The cocktails featured in this book are given names that are carefully curated to evoke a sense of light-hearted eeriness. We believe that the name of a cocktail is an essential component of its enjoyment. We taste first with our eyes, so it's important for a cocktail to not only look appealing but also have a name that conjures up an image that is either intriguing or alluring, or, ideally, both. To create even more of an atmosphere for your cocktail experience, the drinks are organized into themed parts.

Part one exclusively features absinthe cocktails. Absinthe is the one liquor that gets its own section because if you are determined to drink cocktails with ironically macabre names, they might as well incorporate a spirit that was once banned due to supposed toxicity. (It's not toxic, by the way.) Drinking "toxic" cocktails to celebrate life perfectly epitomizes the paradox of jazz funerals as life-affirming celebrations. If you are looking for a cocktail with a specific liquor, refer to the Cocktail Index by Main Spirit on page 136.

Part two focuses on New Orleans cemeteries, exploring their architecture, lore, and libations inspired by the above-ground crypts and tombs. Part three tells a selection of the city's myriad ghost stories and suggests drinks inspired by these eerie tales. Part four is dedicated to vampire-inspired cocktails, which can be enjoyed in the comfort of your own home or in one of the numerous vampire bars located in the city. Part five combines recipes inspired by the practice of Voodoo and witchcraft, both deeply rooted in New Orleans mystical lore.

At the close of each part, you'll find a Haunted History segment, featuring photographs and more in-depth historical and/or supernatural stories connected with each of the cocktails.

In each of the five parts, the recipes are a combination of classic cocktails, unique twists on beloved standards, and fresh, original libations. They are tied together by the narratives they weave about the mystical side of New Orleans. Additionally, some of the recipes include a libation lagniappe. *Lagniappe* (lan-yap) is a Cajun French term meaning "a little something extra," providing bonus tidbits of information and stories about the featured cocktail on that page.

Over the next few pages, you'll find recommendations for essential pantry items, glassware, and recommended liquors to keep in stock. We encourage the use of local New Orleans ingredients whenever possible. Some of these local items, like satsuma, a variety of mandarin orange, are not always available or in season, so, in these situations, we have provided suitable substitutes. Many other local ingredients, however, are shelf-stable and available for purchase all year round through online retailers (alternatively, we list more common substitutes available in most supermarkets). These local ingredients that we recommend are for the times when you feel adventurous, but, by all means, always feel free to use what you have on hand. It's the drinks that are meant to be frightening, not the grocery list.

Our recipes will usually call for local syrups with all-natural ingredients, especially ones made by El Guapo or Cocktail & Sons, which we primarily use. While these brands ship worldwide, feel free to use any syrups that are easily accessible in your area. Several of the featured cocktails also call for a traditional simple syrup, which can be easily purchased at most supermarkets or liquor stores or online. However, if you prefer to make your own simple syrup, infused syrups, or other pantry staples, refer to the recipes on pages 12-13.

All cocktails are single-serve unless otherwise noted. Drink ingredients are given in US measurements, but you can refer to the table on page 13 for metric conversions.

Lastly, should you care to visit some of the places mentioned in this book, a Haunted New Orleans Map is included on page 128. There is nothing more agreeable on a cool autumn evening than soaking up the paranormal vibes in a haunted bar. Or restaurant. Or hotel. Choose your adventure; everything in New Orleans is haunted!

SIMPLE SYRUP

Makes 11 ounces

1 CUP WATER

1 CUP GRANULATED SUGAR

Place the water in a medium saucepan and put over medium heat. When the water is hot (no need to bring it to a boil), add the sugar and stir well. Once the sugar has fully dissolved, remove from the heat and let cool to room temperature. It can be stored in an airtight container in the refrigerator for up to 4 weeks.

CINNAMON SIMPLE SYRUP

Makes 32 ounces

2 CUPS WATER

4 CUPS GRANULATED SUGAR

6 CINNAMON STICKS

2 TEASPOONS VANILLA EXTRACT (OPTIONAL)

Place the water and sugar in a large saucepan over medium heat and stir until the sugar is completely dissolved. Remove from the heat and add the cinnamon sticks. Infuse for at least 1 hour or up to 6 hours. Strain out the solids and stir in the vanilla extract, if you like. Cool completely before using. Store in a bottle with a tight seal in the refrigerator for up to 3 weeks.

BASIL SIMPLE SYRUP

Makes 8 ounces

1 CUP WATER

1 CUP GRANULATED SUGAR

10 TO 12 BASIL LEAVES

Place the water and sugar in a small saucepan, stir to combine, and put over medium-high heat. Bring to a boil and remove from the heat. Add in the basil leaves and let steep for 10 to 15 minutes. Using a colander or cheesecloth, strain the liquid into an airtight container. It can be stored in the refrigerator for up to 2 weeks.

CRANBERRY BALSAMIC GASTRIQUE

Makes 8 ounces

½ CUP FRESH CRANBERRIES

¾ CUP BALSAMIC VINEGAR

¼ CUP WATER

1 CUP GRANULATED SUGAR

Combine the cranberries, vinegar, and water in a small saucepan and bring to a boil over high heat. Slowly stir in the sugar, reduce the heat, and let simmer for 20 minutes, stirring occasionally. Strain into a heatproof jar, cool, and refrigerate. It can be stored in an airtight container in the refrigerator for up to 2 weeks.

ORGEAT

Makes 8 ounces

½ GRAPEFRUIT

½ CUP GRANULATED SUGAR

1 CUP ALMOND MILK

8 DROPS ALMOND EXTRACT

4 DROPS ORANGE BLOSSOM WATER

Use a vegetable peeler to peel off the rind of the grapefruit, avoiding the bitter white pith. Place the sugar and grapefruit peel in a medium airtight container. Let it sit until the citrus oils have begun to soak into the sugar (the sugar will look wet), about 2 hours at room temperature. Remove the peel and add the almond milk, almond extract, and orange blossom water, then seal the container and shake until the sugar dissolves. It can be stored in an airtight container in the refrigerator for up to 1 week.

LIQUID MEASUREMENT CONVERSION TABLE

FLUID OUNCES	CUPS/TABLESPOONS	METRIC
16 OUNCES	2 CUPS	480 MILLILITERS
12 OUNCES	1½ CUPS	360 MILLILITERS
8 OUNCES	1 CUP	240 MILLILITERS
6 OUNCES	¾ CUP	180 MILLILITERS
5 OUNCES	1 CUP + 2 TABLESPOONS	150 MILLILITERS
4 OUNCES	½ CUP	120 MILLILITERS
3 OUNCES	6 TABLESPOONS	90 MILLILITERS
2 OUNCES	¼ CUP	60 MILLILITERS
1 OUNCE	⅛ CUP / 2 TABLESPOONS	30 MILLILITERS
¾ OUNCE	1½ TABLESPOONS	22.5 MILLILITERS
½ OUNCE	1 TABLESPOON	15 MILLILITERS

→ WICKED WARES ←
GLASSWARE & PANTRY RECOMMENDATIONS

Cocktails are tasty and artful luxuries, so the elements that compose them, from the ingredients to the serving vessels, form the cornerstone of cocktail crafting. An exceptional cocktail experience engages the senses. In addition to tasting delicious, cocktails should be visually appealing, feel good in your hand, and fit the occasion. So for the best experience, stock an array of spirits, mixers, garnishes, and glassware. Below are a few recommendations to get you started.

GLASSWARE

COUPE GLASS: The wide rim evokes a chic retro feel that translates to the cocktail (and makes you feel so bougie).

CHAMPAGNE FLUTE: Use a flute when you serve champagne or Prosecco; the straight sides reduce the amount of oxygen that gets into the glass, making the bubbles last longer.

MARTINI GLASS: Glassware doesn't get more classic than a martini glass; it never goes out of style and will give your drink a cosmopolitan vibe.

HIGHBALL GLASS: Use these to serve tall cocktails and other mixed drinks containing a large proportion of nonalcoholic mixers, especially carbonated ones poured over ice.

LOWBALL GLASS: Sometimes referred to as old-fashioned glasses, lowball glasses are essentially shorter versions of highball glasses. They are perfect for when you want to highlight the liqueur in your cocktail or drink it neat or on the rocks.

MULE TIN: This copper mug is best used for cocktail recipes that call for beer because the metal insulates and helps maintain the cool temperature. No one likes hot beer!

PUNCH GLASS: These petite cups nestle around your punchbowl, so the crowd can sip your brew with perfect portions.

HURRICANE GLASS: These glasses' 20-ounce capacity makes them ideal for tropical drinks that include multiple juices and garnishes.

Mix-Ins

BITTERS: A good New Orleans cocktail calls for Peychaud's Bitters. Antoine Amédée Peychaud was an apothecary in the French Quarter in the early nineteenth century, and his bitters were used to make New Orleans Sazeracs. Also, try out El Guapo Bitters, another New Orleans favorite made locally in myriad inventive flavors like gumbo and crawfish boil.

TABASCO SAUCE: If you're not using it in your Bloody Marys, you should at least be using it on your food. A spicy kick enhances flavors across the board.

CHERRIES: Consider maraschino, brandy- or bourbon-soaked, or black, according to your preference. Regardless of your choice, cherries make your cocktail more enticing by adding visual appeal and a pop of color.

ACID PHOSPHATE: This tangy soda will leave a tongue-tingling sensation in your mouth. It enhances the sour character of cocktails and adds some fun fizz.

CLARET SYRUP: This is a wine syrup that works with cocktails and desserts alike! Made of equal parts red wine and simple syrup, adding claret brings in a sophisticated sweet layer to any cocktail.

GARNISHES: Lemons, limes, oranges (blood oranges and satsumas are preferable because they grow locally), cinnamon sticks, and fresh mint elevate the flavors of New Orleans nicely. If you are making a Cajun Bloody Mary, you will need to make a full-on grocery run.

Liqueurs

BÉNÉDICTINE: Herbal and spicy with citrus notes and a hint of pine, the recipe for Bénédictine is a closely guarded trade secret known by only a handful of people at any given time to preserve the Renaissance mystique. But even those not in the loop know that Bénédictine pairs beautifully with bourbon.

COINTREAU: An iconic orange liqueur, this type of Triple Sec can be used in an array of cocktails, from margaritas to cosmopolitans.

CRÈME DE VIOLETTE: This liqueur adds violet flower flavoring to brandy. Its floral sweetness can be enjoyed alone as a cordial by brandy lovers or served with dry vermouth.

ST-GERMAIN ELDERFLOWER LIQUEUR: A French liqueur made from fresh elderflowers, its notes of pear, peach, and grapefruit add to the floral flavor making it the perfect addition to your gin and tonic or Corpse Reviver.

CRÈME DE CACAO: This sweet chocolate-bean liqueur scented with vanilla was first made by monks in the 1600s after cocoa beans were brought back to Europe from America. It is used in the classic New Orleans cocktails, the Grasshopper, the Brandy Alexander, and the Bushwhacker.

GATOR BITE COFFEE LIQUEUR & RUM: An infused black coffee liqueur with a decadent dark chocolate taste, this liqueur has hazelnut and toffee notes that are balanced by a hint of citrus.

GATOR BITE SATSUMA & RUM LIQUEUR: This liqueur has a mandarin orange flavor reminiscent of orange sorbet. It's a great addition to margaritas and pairs well with ginger beer.

EVANGELINE'S PRALINES & CREAM: The praline flavor of Evangeline's pays homage to a New Orleans confectionery tradition. This liqueur embraces the sweetness of the classic candy and is an indulgent dessert in a bottle that also makes a suitable substitute for Baileys Irish Cream.

LOCAL SPIRITS

We often suggest local spirits in our recipes. While you're welcome to use what you prefer or have on hand, here's a selection (by no means an exhaustive list) of spirits that you may want to add to your collection. We hope you discover ones that suit your taste.

RUM

CELEBRATION DISTILLATION CRYSTAL RUM: This is for the purists among us. Its smooth, simple flavor is classic, making it a perfect choice for a daiquiri.

CELEBRATION DISTILLATION AMBER RUM: Aged in bourbon barrels made of white oak, this rum is perfect for sipping. It's a rum designed for those who appreciate a smokey, Scotch-like drink. The rum makes a delicious Rum Old Fashioned and can be used in eggnog.

ROULAISON AMBER HERBAL RUM LIQUEUR: This rum liqueur is made from Louisiana sugar and a variety of herbs and is finished with pepper.

CELEBRATION DISTILLATION CAJUN SPICE RUM: If you're a fan of Cajun food, you'll love this rum. It's distilled with seven spices: chicory, clove, cayenne, allspice, nutmeg, ginger, and cinnamon.

CELEBRATION DISTILLATION 121 PROOF RUM: This high-proof rum is the overproof version of the distillery's Crystal Rum, so even though it's not for the faint of heart, you'll still enjoy a smooth and straightforward taste.

ROULAISON BARREL AGED RESERVE RUM: This reserve is aged in barrels formerly used for whiskey or brandy and then transferred to casks to mature.

ROULAISON TRADITIONAL POT DISTILLED RUM: This complex white rum features tropical flavors of banana and pineapple infused with spices.

ROULAISON CANEQUINA APERITIF: A Louisiana-inspired version of a nineteenth-century French quinquina (tonic wine), this aperitif begins with a base of fresh cane juice, and is aromatized with cinchona, gentian, orange peel, and chicory.

BOURBON & WHISKEY

IRISH CHANNEL WHISKEY: All the bourbons and whiskeys from local distillery Seven Three Distilling are named after the neighborhoods in New Orleans. This small-batch blended whiskey pays tribute to the Irish immigrant community. Expect aromas of vanilla wafer, butterscotch pudding, shaved coconut, creamed corn, malt, and fruit. The process of barrel-resting in cognac casks adds additional layers of depth and complexity to the whiskey.

SAZERAC RYE WHISKEY: While this rye whiskey is mostly made in Kentucky, its roots lie in New Orleans. This is the must-use whiskey for the city's signature cocktail, the Sazerac. The flavors of black pepper and clove give rye-based whiskey a spicy flavor that distinguishes it from whiskey made from other grains, such as corn and wheat.

BYWATER BOURBON: Made from Louisiana wheat and corn, this bourbon captures the essence of the Southern heat, infusing unexpected notes of apricot and dried fruit. Its delightful blend of sweet vanilla with undercurrents of mint and chamomile makes for a true sensory experience.

VODKA

NOLA VODKA MARDI GRAS SPECIAL EDITION: This is a smooth vodka with a crisp, fruity profile, and it's perfect for giving your libation (or your coffee on a chilly Mardi Gras morning) an extra shot of fun.

THE ORIGINAL TRINITY VODKA: This vodka by NOLA Distillery pays homage to the three integral ingredients that create the foundation of New Orleans cooking: onions, celery, and bell peppers, collectively known as "the Trinity." These savory flavors make it a perfect choice for a Bloody Mary.

ST. ROCH VODKA: This vodka from Seven Three Distilling undergoes five rounds of distillation and a five-day filtration process, resulting in a premium product that can be enjoyed on its own or mixed into a cocktail. Named for the St. Roch neighborhood, it has a creamy texture with notes of sugarcane in its aroma and a lingering hint of sweetness on the palate.

ST. ROCH CUCUMBER VODKA: This is a good choice when you want a vodka with a fresh, clean taste. It complements sweet, savory, and citrus flavors.

REVERENCE & REVELRY

Why would you want to drink a cocktail whose name implies it will do you in? Most people wouldn't unless they're in the City of the Dead and want to see if New Orleans lives up to its nickname. Drinks like Obituary Cocktail and Death in the Afternoon share more than delightfully macabre names. They both include absinthe, an ingredient shrouded in mystery and misinformation.

Morbidly named absinthe cocktails go over well with residents in a city that celebrates both life and death with equal zeal. Perhaps nowhere is this dichotomy more evident than in the traditions surrounding the jazz funeral. A jazz funeral is a funeral procession led by a brass band to escort the casket and mourners to the cemetery. The trip to the cemetery is mournful and contemplative, but after the interment, the mood turns joyful with the brass band playing upbeat jazz.

All funerals are steeped in ritual as it's important to give the deceased a proper farewell—to celebrate the lives of departed family and friends and send them off to a different, and hopefully better, existence (at the very least, one with less humidity and no hurricanes). Jazz funerals are public parades that blend the conflicted feelings of those left behind: sadness at the loss of a loved one and joy for the transition to that better place.

Starting off somber and ending on a jubilant note, the music of a jazz funeral is representative of the sadness we feel over the departure of a loved one along with the happiness over their present peace. In this context, toasting the departed after their funeral makes sense. These absinthe drinks provide the perfect send-off for a friend or family member who is preceding us on the journey we will all take.

ABSINTHE FRAPPÉ

If symbolism and irony are your thing, all this talk of celebrating life amidst death might just spark your mood for a cocktail with a spirit believed to be detrimental to your health. Good thing absinthe is not actually the hallucinogenic it was once thought to be, especially if you enjoy an absinthe frappé at the Old Absinthe House. After all, you don't need a hallucinogenic to make you see ghosts at that bar; it's the most haunted of all the haunted bars in the city.

1½ OUNCES ABSINTHE

½ OUNCE SIMPLE SYRUP
(PAGE 12)

2 OUNCES SODA WATER

4 OR 5 MINT LEAVES,
PLUS MORE FOR GARNISH
(OPTIONAL)

Fill a cocktail shaker and a glass of your choice with crushed ice. Add the absinthe, syrup, soda water, and mint leaves to the cocktail shaker, then shake gently. Strain into the glass. Garnish with more mint, if desired.

LIBATION LAGNIAPPE

Absinthe was banned in the United States in 1912. The ban was lifted in 2007 due in large part to New Orleanian Ted Breaux, a chemist, environmental microbiologist, and master distiller whose chemical analyses proved that absinthe, if consumed responsibly, was safe.

TRADITIONAL
ABSINTHE
DRIP

This drip dilutes the absinthe and curtails its bitter anise taste while preserving the spirit's full flavor and bouquet. The act of combining absinthe with cold water also results in the louche, or cloudiness, that many absinthe connoisseurs enjoy. This effect is caused by the insoluble ingredients in the absinthe that drop out of the alcohol when combined with water, turning the drink cloudy with a milky opaqueness. If you are looking for a drink with a spectral ambiance, you must try this ritual. There is nothing quite as delightfully eerie as watching the glowy green absinthe transform into a ghostly white concoction. The drip ritual will round out the flavor of the absinthe, but make sure to use ice-cold water for the full effect. The amounts of the ingredients listed here represent our preference, but feel free to adjust them to your taste.

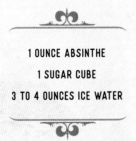

1 OUNCE ABSINTHE

1 SUGAR CUBE

3 TO 4 OUNCES ICE WATER

Pour the absinthe into a glass of your choice. Place a sugar cube on top of a slotted spoon and rest it on the glass. Slowly drip ice-cold water onto the sugar cube, melting it into the glass.

❧ LIBATION LAGNIAPPE ❧

Absinthe—nicknamed "The Green Fairy" due to its mesmerizing color—is a high-proof, anise-flavored liquor, distilled from aromatic plants, particularly wormwood. It derives its signature green color from the chlorophyll released by the herbs.

OBITUARY COCKTAIL

In the spirit of celebrating life with a traditional jazz funeral, how about a cocktail that insinuates you will be next? The Obituary Cocktail is a deadly twist on a dry martini with a lingering flavor of anise. Pastis (a substitute popularized during the ban on absinthe) can be used in place of absinthe if so desired.

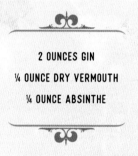

2 OUNCES GIN

¼ OUNCE DRY VERMOUTH

¼ OUNCE ABSINTHE

Fill a cocktail shaker with cracked ice. Add the gin, vermouth, and absinthe, then stir well. Strain into a chilled coupe or martini glass. Make sure your affairs are in order before you take your first sip!

❧ LIBATION LAGNIAPPE ❧

Legend has it the Obituary Cocktail was invented at Lafitte's Blacksmith Shop and you can still order one at this eighteenth-century haunted bar today.

DEATH IN THE AFTERNOON

This absinthe drink was created by Ernest Hemingway who spent quite a bit of time in New Orleans and has a suite at the Hotel Monteleone named after him. In fact, you can enjoy this cocktail in the hotel's whimsical Carousel Bar & Lounge, a rotating bar with a unique design and an ideal place to conclude an evening of ghost touring. However, do watch your step when you leave the bar for your haunted room, as the hotel is known to have many ghosts.

1½ OUNCES ABSINTHE

4½ OUNCES CHILLED
CHAMPAGNE OR PROSECCO

1 LEMON PEEL,
FOR GARNISH (OPTIONAL)

SIMPLE SYRUP (PAGE 12)

Combine the absinthe and champagne or prosecco in a coupe glass and stir well. Garnish with the lemon peel, if desired. To sweeten the death blow, add syrup to taste.

LIBATION LAGNIAPPE

Hemingway's original recipe reads, "Drink three to five of these slowly."
For most mortals, drinking only one or two (slowly) is advisable.

NECROMANCER

Necromancy is the practice of magical sorcery for the purpose of reanimating the dead or foretelling the future. This creepy-sounding absinthe cocktail, created by Chris Hannah for Jewel of the South at the edge of the French Quarter, emphasizes the connection between the living and the dead. If you find yourself in New Orleans around Halloween, be sure to drop in for their spooky cocktails celebrating the season.

1½ OUNCES ABSINTHE

½ OUNCE MADEIRA

¼ OUNCE CRÈME DE VIOLETTE

1 DASH PEYCHAUD'S BITTERS

Place the absinthe, Madeira, crème de violette, and bitters in a wine glass. Stir well and enjoy your new zombie existence.

CORPSE REVIVER

The name says it all. This hair-of-the-dog cocktail has the power to awaken the dead or revive the living after a night of imbibing. With absinthe used only as a glass rinse, it creates a sublimely spooky cocktail for those who like the aroma of absinthe but find its flavor frightening. What better way to end a jazz funeral than with a rousing rendition of "When the Saints Go Marching In" and a corpse reviver?

½ TEASPOON ABSINTHE

1 OUNCE GIN

1 OUNCE LILLET BLANC

1 OUNCE COINTREAU

1 OUNCE FRESH LEMON JUICE

1 LEMON OR ORANGE PEEL, FOR GARNISH

Place the absinthe in a coupe glass. Swirl it around to coat the interior, then discard any excess absinthe; set the glass aside. Fill a cocktail shaker with cracked ice, then add the gin, Lillet Blanc, Cointreau, and juice. Shake vigorously and pour into the absinthe-coated glass. Garnish with either lemon or orange peel.

LIBATION LAGNIAPPE

The Corpse Reviver has been around almost as long as some New Orleans cemeteries. The recipe first appeared in *The Gentleman's Table Guide*, published in 1871. While many bars and restaurants serve this cocktail, our favorite comes from Commander's Palace, across the street from Lafayette Cemetery No. 1 in the Garden District.

LOUISIANA SWAMP THING

Certain Louisiana swamps are thought to be haunted by many mysterious beings, among them the loup-garou (rougarou in Cajun French). This legendary creature is a version of a werewolf, roaming the swamps on full-moon nights. Stories of the rougarou have been told to children around campfires for decades— sometimes by parents at their wits' end looking to scare their kids into good behavior.

1 OUNCE GIN

½ OUNCE ABSINTHE

¼ OUNCE FRESH LIME JUICE

¼ OUNCE SIMPLE SYRUP
(PAGE 12)

1 DASH EL GUAPO CUCUMBER
LAVENDER BITTERS

1 SLICE CUCUMBER, FOR GARNISH

Fill a cocktail shaker with cracked ice. Add the gin, absinthe, juice, syrup, and bitters. Shake vigorously. Strain into a chilled martini or coupe glass and garnish with a cucumber slice.

Looking to add even more atmosphere to your Sazerac? Use dry ice around (not in) your cocktail during the cooler months, or when you just want to add a touch of spookiness to your spirits.

SPOOKY SMOKED SAZERAC

The Sazerac is the signature cocktail of New Orleans, boasting a history of over two hundred years. In a city steeped in tradition, it is fitting that a Sazerac would be served at the celebration of life for a newly departed New Orleanian. While any bar worth its salt will serve a decent Sazerac, the ultimate spot serving this cocktail is the Sazerac Bar nestled within the Roosevelt Hotel—an excellent place to enjoy a seasonal spooky cocktail.

¼ OUNCE ABSINTHE

1 SUGAR CUBE

3 DASHES PEYCHAUD'S BITTERS

1½ OUNCES RYE WHISKEY

1 LEMON PEEL,
FOR GARNISH

1 SPRIG ROSEMARY,
FOR GARNISH

PREPARE A TRADITIONAL SAZERAC: Rinse a chilled lowball glass with absinthe, coat the interior, then discard any excess, and set the glass aside. In a separate lowball glass, add a sugar cube and the bitters. Crush the sugar cube using a muddler. Add the whiskey and 3 ice cubes. Stir. Strain the mixture into the absinthe-coated glass. Garnish with a lemon peel.

NOW SMOKE YOUR SAZERAC: Carefully ignite a rosemary sprig with a culinary torch or a lighter until it begins to smoke. Place the smoking sprig in (smoking side up) or over the glass. Let the smoke linger for 15 to 20 seconds, then remove the rosemary sprig before drinking. Note: The smoke from the rosemary is meant to give this cocktail an extra layer of flavor and set it apart from being a traditional Sazerac, but feel free to omit this step if desired.

HAUNTED HISTORY
REVIVAL OF THE FITTEST

Old Absinthe House

Jean Lafitte's Old Absinthe House is the home of the original absinthe frappé and has the added allure of being haunted by the infamous pirate Jean Lafitte, New Orleans's busiest ghost, and Voodoo queen Marie Laveau. This two-hundred-year-old bar was the location of Lafitte's meeting with Andrew Jackson, where the two struck a famous deal during the War of 1812. Patrons have recounted sightings of the pair gathered at a table, sharing a beer. What is consistent in every report of the sightings is that Jean Lafitte is always seen wearing his hat. While most buildings in New Orleans, especially those in the French Quarter, are inhabited by ghosts, the Old Absinthe House stands out as the most haunted. Not only do numerous ghosts dwell here, but they also show up more often. The ghosts here are simply more social!

Belle Époque Absinthe Fountain

During the height of absinthe's popularity, absinthe fountains were featured in bars around town. These beautiful marble fountains were used to drip cool water over sugar into glasses of absinthe, creating a cloudy, spooky drink (see page 23). If you pop into Belle Époque on Bourbon Street, you can see the original fountain from the Old Absinthe Bar, which was hidden away during Prohibition and moved to this location after its repeal.

Jazz Funerals

Funerals accompanied by brass bands are not exclusive to New Orleans. However, what makes a jazz funeral in New Orleans distinctive is its integration with the second-line parade and dance. During a second line, the participants carry brightly decorated parasols, or if you're joining in late, a handkerchief or paper tissue will do. The key is to joyously sway to the music while waving something overhead; there really aren't too many other rules. As Irma Thomas, dubbed the "Soul Queen of New Orleans," has often explained before performing the second line, it is a dance for all celebratory occasions: weddings, divorces, births, deaths, and a hurricane season without an evacuation.

Because a second line is a parade, there is always a leader. If it's a funeral, the hearse and family of the deceased lead the way. There's always a brass band and parasols, and in a funeral second line, the participants wind through the streets of the Cities of the Dead and back into the streets of the city of the living, symbolizing that while death surrounds us, we are still alive.

Bayou Barataria

Legends from Louisiana's swamps range from hauntings by Voodoo queens to the prowling of otherworldly creatures. It is rumored that pirates considered these marshes, particularly around Bayou Barataria, a perfect hiding place for buried treasure. According to pirate lore, it was customary to kill one of the crewmen and bury the body with the treasure so their spectral presence would serve as a guardian, as a "fifolet." The ghostly sentry appears as a glowing, light-blue ball above the spot where the treasure is buried. Wandering through a swamp is never advisable, especially at night. However, if for some reason you find yourself there and see a blue light, don't dig nearby.

Hotel Monteleone and the Carousel Bar

The Hotel Monteleone is a historic landmark that has consistently earned a spot on nearly every "Best Haunted Hotels in New Orleans" list. Among its famed spectral residents is Maurice Begere, a child ghost whose story dates back to the late 1800s. Maurice's parents loved opera and often stayed at the hotel to attend the productions at the old French Opera House in the French Quarter. Meanwhile, Maurice would stay behind at the hotel with his nanny. One night, Maurice fell ill with a sudden fever. Despite the doctor's efforts, he suffered a convulsion and died in his room on the fourteenth floor. Devastated, his parents returned to the hotel every year on the anniversary of his death in hopes that he would appear. One year, their wish came true when Maurice's mother, Josephine, saw him. Maurice smiled at her and told her to stop worrying about him. Maurice still visits the hotel on a regular basis, and many guests have spotted him—smiling, playful, and harmless—on the 14th floor. Maurice is a reminder that not all ghosts are scary or evil.

The Hotel Monteleone's Carousel Bar is the city's first and only rotating bar. A full rotation takes fifteen minutes, and the bar's intricate carvings and nightly entertainment (Liberace once played here!) make it an exquisite place to enjoy a fantastic cocktail. However, you may not see Maurice there since he's, well, underage.

Jewel of the South

Tucked away at the edge of the French Quarter, the Jewel of the South is the place to relax after a day of cemetery touring. You can enjoy an award-winning cocktail program that embraces local, seasonal flavors. Nestled within an 1830s Creole cottage, this establishment exudes a rich historical ambience, with one of the coziest courtyards in the French Quarter.

COMMANDER'S PALACE

Commander's Palace is the grande dame of Uptown New Orleans restaurants and is the quintessential Uptown Creole restaurant. As any realtor will tell you, topping the list of factors that attract buyers to a property is its location. Evidently, the same holds for attracting ghosts. Located directly across the street from Lafayette Cemetery No. 1, where over seven thousand souls rest, Commander's Palace, unsurprisingly, hosts many ghosts, including the original owner, Emile Commander. He's easily recognizable—a well-dressed man with a handsome mustache, floating from table to table, checking on guests. There's also a young woman often seen on the majestic stairway in the main dining room. Another regular, however, is not so much fun to encounter. She's a very unhappy woman who haunts the ladies' room and has been known to throw objects at people. Add these regulars to the cemetery residents from across the street and you have a very haunted but beautiful restaurant that serves spook-tacular meals.

SAZERAC BAR AT THE ROOSEVELT HOTEL

The Sazerac Bar at the Roosevelt Hotel is the quintessential place to drink New Orleans's official cocktail. Over the years, many famous people, including Judy Garland, Sonny and Cher, and Marilyn Monroe have enjoyed a Sazerac cocktail here. The bar was a men-only establishment, except for Mardi Gras Day when women were admitted. However, on a pivotal September day in 1949, the women of New Orleans stormed the Sazerac, demanding to be let in. The men caved, and since then women were welcome. Now, every September, New Orleans women dress in 1940s fashion and "storm the Sazerac." When we do, we hear the lingering echoes of the women who staged the original rebellion, clearing the way for us to enjoy the beauty of the Sazerac Bar. We can feel their presence and hear their laughter. In a city as haunted as this one, that's not surprising!

CEMETERY SPIRITS

There is a saying that goes, "Here in the South, we don't hide crazy. We parade it on the front porch and give it a cocktail." But it's not just crazy that's on display; we do the same with our deceased with funeral parades and above-ground tombs that have become part of the New Orleans landscape and our daily lives. The familiarity of seeing the generations who have gone before us as part of our day-to-day routines is probably why the (living) residents are perfectly comfortable drinking morbidly named cocktails like The Soggy Grave or The Undertaker.

No visit to New Orleans would be complete without a trip to one of our world-famous cemeteries. Not only is it a great way to get a feel for the history of the city, but it's also the ideal way to work up a thirst for a cocktail. With potential scares around every headstone, throats can get pretty dry with all the shrieking and screaming.

Touring cemeteries to acknowledge those who went before us, followed by cocktails and a meal with those who are still with us, is profoundly life-affirming and a perfect way to spend the day—or the night, if you prefer.

THE
SOGGY GRAVE

It doesn't take much digging to reach water in New Orleans, and early inhabitants of the city struggled to bury their dead in the ground. Coffins, even when weighted with stones or with holes drilled into them, would pop up during heavy rains. Floating coffins became such a problem after Hurricane Katrina that Louisiana mandated identification on all coffins so they could be returned to their original resting place if disturbed. Hopefully, you'll never witness this—just imagining it can make you yearn for a stiff drink.

1½ OUNCES BOURBON

½ OUNCE CLARET SYRUP

1½ OUNCES LILLET BLANC

1 TEASPOON ACID PHOSPHATE

3 DASHES PEYCHAUD'S BITTERS

Fill a cocktail shaker with cracked ice. Add the bourbon, syrup, Lillet Blanc, acid phosphate, and bitters. Shake well and strain into a coupe glass.

LIBATION LAGNIAPPE

This Louisiana spin on a Wet Grave cocktail contains two ingredients that may not be in your bar (but should be): acid phosphate and claret syrup. Acid phosphate brings in a sparkly, carbonated goodness while claret syrup, made of equal parts red wine and simple syrup, adds a sophisticated sweetness to your cocktails.

THE
UNDERTAKER

There are many versions of this cocktail, but if you're an undertaker in one of the Cities of the Dead, you may need a rendition, like this one, that packs enough coffee to help you stay alert for signs of restlessness among the residents. You never know when a spirit may be in need of a stroll. Even if you're just a visitor, this caffeinated cocktail might still be a good way to fend off nightmares after a visit to a cemetery.

3 OUNCES VANILLA VODKA

1 OUNCE CRÈME DE CACAO

1 DASH EL GUAPO SPICED
COCOA BITTERS

1 OUNCE GATOR BITE
COFFEE LIQUEUR & RUM

1 OUNCE CHILLED ESPRESSO

Fill a cocktail shaker with cracked ice. Add the vodka, crème de cacao, bitters, and liqueur. Shake well and strain into a chilled martini glass. Stir in the espresso and serve.

FAMILY MAKES ME CRAN-KY

SERVES 25 SOULS

When you visit a New Orleans cemetery, observe how the names of those interred are inscribed not only on the front but also on the sides of the tombs. Family crypts here house many generations. Imagine being buried with everyone in your family who has died since the 1800s! You'd better be prepared to listen to their stories for an eternity, and you might just need a large-batch cocktail like this one, shared with us by Roulaison Distilling.

1 GALLON WATER

8 CINNAMON APPLE SPICE TEA BAGS
(SUCH AS CELESTIAL SEASONINGS)

1 QUART (32 OUNCES) CINNAMON SIMPLE SYRUP
(PAGE 12)

2 BOTTLES (750 ML EACH) ROULAISON
TRADITIONAL POT DISTILLED RUM

1 QUART (32 OUNCES) CRANBERRY
POMEGRANATE JUICE (SUCH AS L&A BRAND)

1½ QUARTS (48 OUNCES) CRANBERRY JUICE
(SUCH AS L&A BRAND)

⅓ CUP FRESH LIME JUICE

1 LITER (33.8 OUNCES) GINGER BEER
(SUCH AS GOSLING'S)

2 TEASPOONS EL GUAPO
HOLIDAY PIE BITTERS

Place the water in a 5-quart pot and bring to a boil over high heat. Remove from the heat and drop in the tea bags. Steep for at least 30 minutes and up to 45 minutes. Remove the tea bags, then leave the tea to cool completely. Add the tea and syrup to a large mixing bowl with the rum, juices, ginger beer, and bitters. Stir thoroughly and chill in the refrigerator before serving in ice-filled lowball glasses.

SUFFERING BASTARD

Some poor souls buried in these tombs are stuck for eternity with relatives they tried to avoid in life. That calls for hard liquor with a dash of bitters. So, raise a glass in honor of your second cousin Fred, who was just buried but, instead of enjoying his peaceful rest, is now stuck listening to Aunt Lucille, the hypochondriac, detailing every single one of her many ailments. Here's to the suffering bastard!

4 OUNCES GINGER BEER

1 OUNCE DRY GIN

1 OUNCE BRANDY

½ OUNCE FRESH LIME JUICE

¼ OUNCE SIMPLE SYRUP
(PAGE 12)

2 DASHES PEYCHAUD'S BITTERS

1 SPRIG MINT, FOR GARNISH

Fill a highball glass with cracked ice and add the ginger beer. Fill a cocktail shaker with cracked ice, then add the gin, brandy, juice, syrup, and bitters. Shake well and strain into the highball glass. Garnish with the mint sprig.

LIBATION LAGNIAPPE

The Suffering Bastard was invented during World War II by chemist-turned-bartender Joe Scialom at a bar in Cairo, a popular spot among British soldiers. Scialom created the drink as a hangover cure, which is often needed in New Orleans.

CEMETERY ANGEL

The essence of this drink evokes the imagery of angels often found in cemetery art. These graceful angels symbolize concepts like rebirth, resurrection, protection, judgment, wisdom, mercy, or divine love depending on their depictions. Clasped hands, for example, represent farewell and hope, while hands pointing downward invoke the Earth as a witness and upward-pointing hands show the pathway to heaven. Cemetery art speaks a poignant and beautiful language of its own, and it's these beautiful angels in our historic cemeteries that inspire this cocktail.

1 TABLESPOON LIGHT BROWN SUGAR

2 DASHES PEYCHAUD'S BITTERS

½ OUNCE SATSUMA OR BLOOD ORANGE JUICE

1 OUNCE ANGEL'S ENVY BOURBON

2 OUNCES CLUB SODA

Place the brown sugar in a lowball glass. Add the bitters and juice and stir until the sugar fully dissolves. Add the bourbon and stir to combine. Add ice cubes and top with the club soda.

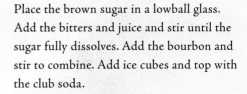

LIBATION LAGNIAPPE

In Louisiana, satsumas begin ripening in late September, aligning perfectly with Spooky Season for this recipe. Don't fret if you can't get your hands on this elusive citrus; fresh blood orange juice makes a fine substitute.

A caveau is also a small
cellar—the kind you want
to use for storing wine and
liquors, not bodies. That
said, a deep, dark, autumnal
cocktail with fruit notes
may be in order after your
cemetery visit. This recipe
creates enough
to share with all your
future caveau-mates!

CAVEAU COCKTAIL

SERVES 8–10 SOULS

This cocktail, with its host of ingredients, is appropriately named after the section of the tomb that houses many remains. Most New Orleans tombs have two shelves for coffins and an open area at the bottom known as the caveau (French for "cave"). When a new casket is placed in the crypt, the remains in the bottom-shelf casket are transferred to the caveau and the coffin is burned. The top casket is moved to the bottom shelf, the newly dead is put on top, and the cycle continues throughout time. The result is the intermingling of bones from different individuals, blending the spirits together in the caveau.

1 BOTTLE (750 ML) RED WINE (ANY VARIETY)

1 CUP FRESH BLACKBERRIES, PREFERABLY LOUISIANA–GROWN

5 WHOLE CLOVES

3 PODS STAR ANISE, PLUS MORE FOR GARNISH

2 CINNAMON STICKS, PLUS MORE FOR GARNISH

1 SATSUMA, PEELED AND SEPARATED INTO PIECES

1 CUP APPLE CIDER

½ CUP BRANDY

½ CUP LOUISIANA CANE SYRUP (SUCH AS STEEN'S)

PEYCHAUD'S BITTERS, FOR FINISHING

Place the wine, blackberries, cloves, star anise, cinnamon, satsuma, apple cider, brandy, and syrup in a medium heavy-bottomed Dutch oven or stainless-steel saucepan. Cover with the lid and bring to a gentle simmer over medium heat, making sure to never let the liquid come to a hard boil, for 30 to 60 minutes, until the mixture starts to thicken. Remove from the heat and strain into heatproof lowball glasses or mugs. Garnish each serving with a cinnamon stick and star anise pod and finish with a dash of bitters.

CITIES OF THE DEAD

Small neighborhood cemeteries are abundant in New Orleans, and each one tells its own story. Not all cemeteries are as famous as St. Louis No. 1, but all the residents in the Cities of the Dead have stories to tell. Wandering the streets of the Cities of the Dead, reading tomb inscriptions as you stroll, is a fascinating way to connect with those who have come before us.

½ OUNCE TRIPLE SEC

½ OUNCE OLD NEW ORLEANS 121 PROOF RUM

½ OUNCE ST. ROCH VODKA

½ OUNCE GENTILLY GIN

½ OUNCE TEQUILA

½ OUNCE IRISH CHANNEL WHISKEY

½ OUNCE SCOTCH

1 CAN (12 OUNCES) AMBER LAGER BEER
(SUCH AS ABITA AMBER)

1 CAN (16 OUNCES) IRISH STOUT BEER
(SUCH AS NOLA BREWING IRISH CHANNEL STOUT)

Add the triple sec, rum, vodka, gin, tequila, whiskey, and Scotch to a beer mug or mule tin and stir to combine. Fill to the top with equal parts lager and stout.

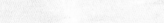

LIBATION LAGNIAPPE

This is our New Orleans version of the Graveyard Cocktail, made with locally sourced products named for popular neighborhoods St. Roch, Gentilly, and the Irish Channel. Be forewarned—this is one of the strongest libations out there, and it's not for the faint of heart.

DEADLY VIPERS

This cocktail lives up to its name; it packs a wallop and might just send you to an early grave! In the spirit of deadly libations, head to Palm & Pine at the edge of the French Quarter and only a few blocks away from St. Louis No. 1, one of the oldest cemeteries in New Orleans. Created by beverage director Kimberly Patton-Bragg, the Guanábana (soursop) purée gives this cocktail a fruity, citrus taste, complementing the aged sweetness of the Macchu Pisco brandy.

1½ OUNCES MACCHU PISCO BRANDY

¼ OUNCE MARASCHINO LIQUEUR

1 OUNCE GUANÁBANA PURÉE

½ OUNCE FRESH LIME JUICE

2 HEAVY DASHES ALLSPICE DRAM

MARASCHINO CHERRIES
(SUCH AS LUXARDO), FOR GARNISH

LIME WEDGE, FOR GARNISH

Fill a cocktail shaker with cracked ice. Add the brandy, liqueur, purée, juice, and dram. Shake well and pour with the ice into a highball glass. Garnish with cherries and a lime wedge.

HAUNTED HISTORY
TOMB TIME

St. Louis Cemetery No. 1

One of New Orleans's most haunted locations, St. Louis No. 1 was established in the 1700s to replace an earlier cemetery within the area now known as the French Quarter. The cemetery was built outside the city's ramparts to reduce the spread of diseases. Still in use today, St. Louis No. 1 houses some significant figures, including Marie Laveau, the most renowned New Orleans Voodoo priestess. Among the notable future residents is actor Nicolas Cage, who has constructed here a rather stark pyramid tomb awaiting his eventual demise.

Lafayette Cemetery No. 1

Yellow fever took a heavy toll on New Orleans in the nineteenth century, and if you look at the graves in Lafayette No. 1 in the Garden District, it's easy to see that impact. Most of the tomb inscriptions bear witness to loved ones lost in droves to the disease. Lafayette No. 1 is also the epicenter for witches and vampires, serving as the burial ground for Anne Rice's fictional Mayfair witches and a popular filming location for several movies, notably—and appropriately—*Interview with the Vampire*. All the activities of these film and television shoots definitely provide the souls here with some entertainment. However, if you ask most of the residents, they would say haunting the famed Commander's Palace across the street is a more fun way to kill boredom.

St. Louis Cemetery No. 3

Because eating is such an event in New Orleans, the city has an embarrassment of riches when it comes to great chefs. It has been said that while people everywhere else eat to live, in New Orleans, we live to eat! So, it shouldn't be a surprise that foodies have a special place to go to honor departed chefs: Chef's Corner in St. Louis Cemetery No. 3 in the Mid-City neighborhood. It is the final resting place for many renowned New Orleans chefs, including Paul Prudhomme, Jean Galatoire, Guillaume Tujague, and Leah Chase. This cemetery is also the resting grounds for many priests. We aren't sure if it's the chefs or the priests who are still hanging around, but both people who live in the neighborhood and passersby have reported seeing glowing orbs floating along the cemetery pathways.

The Cemeteries Streetcar Line

Most New Orleanians plan ahead on where they want to take up residence in the Cities of the Dead when the time comes. Many will end up at the intersection of Canal Street and City Park Avenue, a spot with multiple cemeteries and mausoleums. In fact, you can ride a streetcar that runs from the heart of the city along Canal Street, officially designated as the Canal-Cemeteries line, but commonly referred to as "The Cemeteries Streetcar Line," concluding at the Cemeteries Transit Terminal. This cluster of cemeteries is memorialized in the song "At the Foot of Canal Street" by John Boutté and Paul Sanchez, with the refrain's final line stating, "I'm going to put on my golden crown at the foot of Canal Street."

METAIRIE CEMETERY

Metairie Cemetery is one of the cemeteries at the foot of Canal Street. Originally, the cemeteries here were on the banks of Bayou Metairie, which once meandered through this area. Featuring lofty, ornate tombs with serpentine tree-shaded pathways, the cemetery is home to several local celebrities, like many kings of Mardi Gras, Tom Bensen, former owner of the New Orleans Saints, and David Hennessey, the nineteenth-century police chief, who met an unfortunate fate after a clash with the local Mafia. His spirit now patrols the cemetery in his police uniform.

GREENWOOD CEMETERY

Greenwood Cemetery houses several notable monuments, including the Firemen's Monument and the Elk's Tumulus, or Elk's Tomb. This is the final resting place of the author John Kennedy Toole, known for his Pulitzer Prize–winning novel, *A Confederacy of Dunces*, which offers a hilarious account of the many characters that make up New Orleans society. Many people have reported seeing his ghost strolling through the cemetery.

HURRICANE KATRINA MEMORIAL AND CHARITY HOSPITAL CEMETERY

With its name evoking traumatic memories, most New Orleanians simply refer to Hurricane Katrina as "The Storm." Standing prominently at the foot of Canal Street is the Hurricane Katrina Memorial, marking a defining moment in New Orleans history. The memorial takes the form of a circle, mirroring the shape of a hurricane. In the center, representing the eye of the storm, a plaque commemorates the date and the failure of the levee system and pays tribute to the more than 1,100 souls lost.

The Hurricane Katrina Memorial is located in close proximity to the Charity Hospital Cemetery where the indigent who died in Charity Hospital are buried. The hospital was shuttered after The Storm inflicted irreparable damage. It serves as the resting ground for 86 individuals, nameless and unclaimed, who lost their lives during the hurricane.

St. Roch Cemetery

The beautiful Gothic mortuary chapel in this 150-year-old cemetery is adorned with discarded crutches, leg braces, and various items left behind by those healed through the intercession of St. Roch, the patron saint of dogs and invalids. This Majorican Catholic confessor lived in the fourteenth century and his intercession was invoked by plague victims. His cemetery is generally off the tourist radar, but it is still haunted. Maybe the ghosts feel more comfortable roaming around where it's less crowded. The most well-known ghost is a hooded figure frequently seen walking through the cemetery walls. Another long-time resident ghost is a large black dog, wandering among the graves and vanishing mysteriously when cornered.

All Saints' Day

On November 1st, Catholics observe All Saints' Day, known as La Toussaint in French. In New Orleans, this day is dedicated to honoring those who have passed away by cleaning their tombs and bringing them flowers. Of course, this being New Orleans, the day is a social event. In earlier times, families would spend the day cleaning and restoring the tombs and picnicking in the graveyard. And because no good celebration should end too soon, the remembrance festivities continue into the next day, November 2nd, known as All Souls' Day, creating a super-sized party for both the living and the dead!

GHOSTS & HAUNTED LIBATIONS

New Orleans is a city inhabited by colorful characters, both living and dead. As a haunted city, encounters with ghosts are not uncommon here. Maybe it's the combination of cultures, religions, and ethnicities that make spirits want to linger after death. Maybe it's just something in the aura and mystical quality of this three-hundred-year-old city that allows the dead to connect with the living more easily. Whatever the reason, New Orleans ghosts are many, varied, and active.

The average house-haunting spirits aren't famous; they're just everyday individuals trying to live their afterlives in peace. However, a few are legendary, like Jean Lafitte, the notorious privateer, and Marie Laveau, the famous Voodoo queen, who have been spotted at multiple locations throughout the French Quarter.

Here's the tricky part about discussing haunted spots in the French Quarter: pretty much the whole neighborhood is haunted. The place is lousy with spirits— and not just the high-proof kind. No self-respecting New Orleans bar or restaurant of a certain age would be without a ghost. Our advice is to have a seat at a table or pull a stool up to a bar in one of these locations and just enjoy whatever classic New Orleans cocktail speaks to you, makes your hair stand on end, or sends chills down your spine. If the idea of drinking in a haunted bar sounds too intimidating, start slow and indulge in these hauntingly delightful cocktails at home while you read a NOLA ghost tale or two.

EVIL WOMAN SHOOTER

The brutal treatment of enslaved people by Madame LaLaurie, a decidedly evil woman who lived in the French Quarter in the 1830s, was brought to light after a house fire. Upon the discovery of this cruelty, an infuriated mob destroyed the home, causing LaLaurie to flee the city and never return. But the remains of the home endured, serving as host to the ghost of a girl who jumped to her death from a balcony rather than face LaLaurie's cruel whip after she pulled her hair while brushing it. This shooter is crafted as a reminder to never forget the horrors and mistakes of the past and, more importantly, to never let them repeat in the future.

½ OUNCE EVANGELINE'S PRALINES & CREAM

½ OUNCE GATOR BITE COFFEE LIQUEUR & RUM

Place the liqueurs in a shot glass. Stir lightly and enjoy!

LIBATION LAGNIAPPE

This quick and simple recipe leans into New Orleans's local spirits. However, Baileys Irish Cream and a hazelnut liqueur, like Frangelico, or an amaretto, like Disaronno, would be equally yummy substitutes.

WHITE GHOST MARTINI

*This sweet cocktail with a dash of bitters is reminiscent of the story of Julie,
the mistress of a wealthy Frenchman in nineteenth-century New Orleans. One cold
December night, the Frenchman promised Julie that if she completely disrobed and went on
the roof as an act of her undying love, he would marry her. He was only joking, but poor
Julie took the challenge seriously. The Frenchman later found her lifeless body on the roof;
Julie had frozen to death waiting for her proposal. Her ghost now appears every year
on a chilly night in December, earning her the nickname the "Clockwork Ghost."
Since Julie never got to wear that white wedding dress, this one's for her!*

1½ OUNCES WHIPPED CREAM VODKA

1 OUNCE WHITE CHOCOLATE LIQUEUR

2 OUNCES HEAVY CREAM, WHOLE MILK,
OR ANY PLANT—BASED MILK

1 DASH EL GUAPO CHICORY PECAN BITTERS

Fill a cocktail shaker with cracked ice.
Add the vodka, liqueur, cream or milk,
and bitters. Shake and strain into a
martini glass.

GHOSTLY EMBRACE

Embrace the exquisite combination of sweet ice cream and smooth vodka in this hauntingly decadent twist on a White Russian. It's a fitting libation to tell the tale of the haunted tomb of Josie Arlington, the notorious New Orleans madam. Reports of strange occurrences began circulating immediately after Josie's burial, including tales of a statue leaving her tomb and wandering around the cemetery. The hordes of curious people that came to the gravesite to investigate claimed to have seen the two torches atop the tomb glow with a mysterious red flame, thus cementing the spooky story of Josie as a legend for the ages.

4 OUNCES VODKA

4 OUNCES CRÈME DE CACAO OR GATOR BITE COFFEE LIQUEUR & RUM

1 SMALL SCOOP VANILLA ICE CREAM (SUCH AS NEW ORLEANS ICE CREAM COMPANY)

GROUND NUTMEG, FOR SPRINKLING

Place the vodka and crème de cacao in a cocktail shaker and set aside. Place the ice cream in a coupe glass and slowly pour the vodka mixture over it. Sprinkle with a pinch of nutmeg and serve immediately.

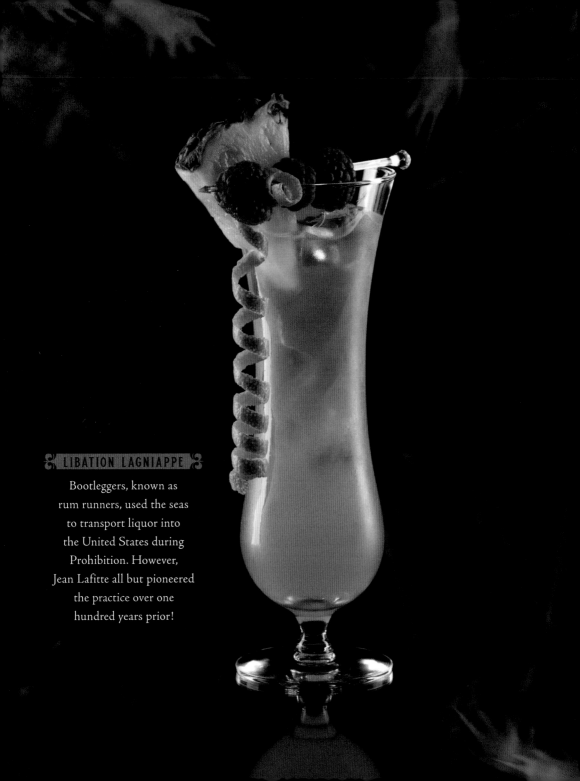

THE PRIVATEER

This New Orleans version of the Rum Runner pays homage to the city's most notorious pirate ghost, Jean Lafitte, who smuggled more than his fair share of rum into New Orleans. His original haunt is one of the oldest bars in the French Quarter, Lafitte's Blacksmith Shop Bar. Tales of the haunted nature of this place are legendary. They range from stories of glowing red eyes emanating from dark corners to sightings of the ghost of Lafitte dressed as a sailor.

1 OUNCE OLD NEW ORLEANS CAJUN SPICED RUM

1 OUNCE GATOR BITE SATSUMA & RUM LIQUEUR

½ OUNCE CRÈME DE CASSIS

½ OUNCE CRÈME DE BANANE

½ OUNCE CRÈME DE MÛR

1 OUNCE SATSUMA OR BLOOD ORANGE JUICE

1 OUNCE PINEAPPLE JUICE

½ OUNCE FRESH LIME JUICE

1 DASH EL GUAPO POYLNESIAN KISS BITTERS

BRANDIED CHERRIES, FOR GARNISH

PINEAPPLE WEDGE, FOR GARNISH

ORANGE PEEL, FOR GARNISH

FRESH RASPBERRIES, FOR GARNISH

Fill a cocktail shaker and a hurricane glass with cracked ice. Add the rums, liqueurs, juices, and bitters to the cocktail shaker. Shake vigorously, then strain into the hurricane glass. Garnish with cherries, pineapple, orange peel, and raspberries.

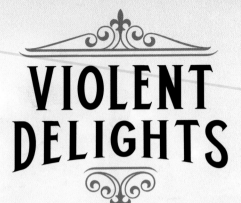

VIOLENT DELIGHTS

This recipe is courtesy of Vessel, a restaurant housed in a former church. Stories of supernatural happenings have circulated since its restoration after Hurricane Katrina. A security camera once caught a bright orb wandering around the patio during the night. It is believed the main spirit haunting Vessel is the Baroness de Pontalba, the former owner of the land on which the church was built. Things got so bad that the waitstaff refused to use the haunted stairs, prompting the chef to call for an exorcism. (Spoiler: It didn't work.)

½ OUNCE FRESH LIME JUICE

½ OUNCE SIMPLE SYRUP (PAGE 12)

½ OUNCE PEAR LIQUEUR

½ OUNCE AMARO ABANO

1½ OUNCES SCOTCH

3 OUNCES GINGER BEER

1 LIME SLICE, FOR GARNISH

Combine and stir the juice, syrup, liqueur, Amaro Abano and Scotch in a mule tin. Add crushed ice and top with ginger beer. Garnish with the lime slice.

LIBATION LAGNIAPPE

Amaro Abano is an herbal liqueur dating back to the 1800s when it was originally sold as a health tonic. While it can be enjoyed as an aperitif, straight or over ice, mixologists are increasingly using the liqueur as a base for cocktails.

MISTAKES
WERE MADE

Some cocktails put you in a contemplative mood. And this one, courtesy of Vessel Restaurant, certainly makes us think of the haunted Beauregard-Keyes House. P. G. T. Beauregard, the Confederate general whose shot ignited the Civil War, inadvertently took thousands of lives in the 1862 Battle of Shiloh when he mistakenly thought the battle was won and ordered a halt. His tactical mistake cost the lives of many young men and boys and brought him profound guilt with which his spirit is apparently still struggling. Believed to reenact the battle in the dark of night in his former home, General Beauregard's spectral presence emerges amidst the sounds of cannons and the scent of gunpowder, muttering the word "Shiloh." This drink serves as a solemn reminder not to repeat mistakes you have made in the past.

¾ OUNCE STRAWBERRY OR TROPICAL FRUIT SYRUP
(SUCH AS COCKTAIL & SONS FASSIONOLA SYRUP)

¾ OUNCE FRESH LEMON JUICE

½ OUNCE AMARO ABANO

1½ OUNCES VODKA

1 LEMON WHEEL, FOR GARNISH

1 STRAWBERRY SLICE, FOR GARNISH

Fill a cocktail shaker with crushed ice. Add the syrup, juice, Amaro Abano, and vodka. Shake vigorously then pour into a highball glass. Garnish with the lemon wheel and strawberry slice.

DRUNK GHOST

New Orleans will always overflow with spirits—both the haunting or the drinking kind—and those spirits can be raucous. Whether it's the spectral pirate party sometimes spotted on the second floor of Absinthe House or the table set each night with a glass of wine for the resident ghost of Muriel's Jackson Square, many haunted French Quarter establishments embrace their ghosts. After all, some specters are the "life" of the party.

WHITE ICING, FOR GARNISH (OPTIONAL)

WHITE SUGAR SPRINKLES, FOR GARNISH (OPTIONAL)

2 OUNCES ROULAISON TRADITIONAL POT DISTILLED RUM

1 OUNCE MARDI GRAS VODKA

2 OUNCES PINEAPPLE JUICE

1 OUNCE SWEETENED COCONUT CREAM

WHIPPED CREAM, FOR GARNISH (OPTIONAL)

If desired, coat the rim of a highball glass with icing, then roll it in sugar sprinkles. Fill the glass with ice cubes and fill the cocktail shaker with cracked ice. Add the rum, vodka, juice, and coconut cream to the cocktail shaker. Shake until well blended. Strain into the prepared glass and top with a dollop of whipped cream, if desired, for an extra hit of spooky sweetness.

LIBATION LAGNIAPPE

Although you can use any rum you like in this recipe, we prefer Roulaison Traditional Pot Distilled Rum made from Louisiana sugarcane. *Roulaison* is the French-Creole term for the sugarcane harvest, and this rum has a robust taste with notes including pineapple, banana, and cinnamon.

LULU WHITE'S BLOODY KNIFE

This creepy cocktail is named after Lulu White, an African American madam infamous for attacking her customers with a knife if they failed to pay for services rendered. Lulu owned Mahogany Hall, a grand home and popular brothel in Storyville, New Orleans's former legalized red-light district. Storyville no longer exists, but many claim the buildings that once housed these brothels, including Lulu White's former abode, are haunted.

1 LIME SLICE, FOR GARNISH

PEYCHAUD'S BITTERS, FOR GARNISH

2 OUNCES 100% AGAVE SILVER TEQUILA

1 OUNCE APEROL

2 OUNCES FRESH RUBY RED GRAPEFRUIT JUICE

½ OUNCE FRESH LIME JUICE

2 OUNCES CLUB SODA

Place the lime slice in a small bowl, add enough bitters to fully cover it, and leave it to soak. Fill a cocktail shaker halfway with cracked ice. Add the tequila, Aperol, and juices. Shake well and strain into a highball glass. Add the club soda, stir, and garnish with the prepared "bloody" lime slice.

LIBATION LAGNIAPPE

Lulu White cocktails are served not only at bars throughout the French Quarter but even as far as Paris. Our rendition is inspired by the one served by Waites Laseter, bartender at hometown haunt Mahogany Jazz Hall.

HAUNTED HISTORY
SUPERNATURAL SELECTION

LaLaurie House

One of the most famous haunted houses in New Orleans, this was the home of the prominent couple Dr. and Madame LaLaurie, who harbored a terrible secret. On April 10, 1834, a fire broke out at the home, revealing the bodies of seven enslaved people, mutilated, and seemingly tortured. The citizens of New Orleans were outraged by this cruelty and chased the LaLauries out of town. Remaining vacant for many years, no one could bear to live in the house given the pain and suffering it represented. The LaLaurie mansion has since been restored and is currently a private residence again, but the house's most famous spirit, the young girl who threw herself off the balcony to escape punishment by Madame LaLaurie, still haunts the courtyard below.

The Sultan's Palace

In the mid-nineteenth century, a man from Turkey came to New Orleans and rented a mansion in the French Quarter. The Sultan brought with him considerable wealth in jewels and gold and lived a lavish lifestyle, with reports of harems and opium dens as standard fare. This all ended gruesomely one fateful night when neighbors noticed blood seeping out from the mansion's iron gates, alluding to a horrific scene: the Sultan's entourage and harem had been murdered and mutilated and the Sultan himself was found in his own garden, buried alive. The perpetrators were never apprehended. That ended the Sultan's reign, but it began the haunting of the Sultan's Palace. The home was subsequently converted to apartments, and over the years residents have reported hearing disembodied footsteps and screaming from unknown sources.

Julie's Royal Street House

Julie, the Clockwork Ghost, is arguably the most reliable ghost in New Orleans, appearing every December on the roof of her former home where she died on that cold, damp night, hoping to get the one thing she wanted most in life: a wedding ring from her beloved. In addition to her winter roof hauntings, Julie has often been seen throughout the year in the building and courtyard, sometimes accompanied by her cat.

Muriel's Jackson Square

A fine-dining restaurant with a ghost story (or two) to tell, Muriel's keeps a table set for their resident spirit, Pierre Antoine Lepardi Jourdan. Jourdan built his dream home at this location but lost it in a poker game in 1814. Overcome by despair, he committed suicide on the second floor, the current site of Muriel's Seance Lounges, which Jourdan frequently haunts, appearing as an orb. Muriel's is also home to a mischievous ghost who inhabits the Courtyard Bar, and has a proclivity for hurling glasses.

Josie's Tomb

Josie Arlington ran one of the most opulent brothels in Storyville. She decided that, upon her death, she wanted to continue mingling with the elite of the city, so she had an ornate tomb constructed as her resting place in Metairie Cemetery. The tomb features a life-size statue of a woman holding a bouquet of flowers, knocking on the door of the tomb and seemingly denied entry, meant to symbolize a young woman being turned away from Josie's brothel because she was a virgin. (Josie liked to brag that no girl had ever lost her virginity in the Arlington house.) Soon after Josie's burial, witnesses reported seeing the statue wander away from its spot, strolling around the cemetery. There were also accounts of the two torches atop the tomb glowing with a red flame. Shortly after these claims, Josie's tomb was sold, and her remains were reburied in an undisclosed location within the cemetery.

MAY BAILY'S PLACE

Most of the grand houses of Storyville were demolished in the 1930s and '40s, however, you can still visit one of the first Storyville bordellos. Now transformed into a bar, this Creole-style cottage pays homage to its past as a brothel with a red light and framed copy of May Baily's 1857 operating license, considered to be the first licensed brothel in New Orleans. Patrons have claimed to see the reflection of one of the courtesans, lingering near the bar, but the best-known ghost is May's sister Millie. Millie yearned to leave the brothel life behind. She fell in love and was to be married, but her beloved died before they could wed. Millie, nicknamed "The Lost Bride," still roams the bar and hotel, occasionally appearing in her wedding dress and veil, forever searching for her long-lost love.

VESSEL RESTAURANT

The Vessel building started as a church and still retains the beautiful architecture of the original structure. It underwent a massive renovation following Hurricane Katrina and almost immediately the owners claimed to be up against some supernatural obstacles, from strange noises to sightings of shadowy figures. Their surveillance camera captured video of an orb on the property that has been identified by *The Dead Files*, a paranormal investigation television show, as none other than eighteenth-century business owner Micaela Almonester, known as the Baroness de Pontalba. In life, even though she was a wealthy and influential aristocrat who played a role in shaping the artistic look of the French Quarter, the Baroness suffered at the hands of her husband and her father-in-law, the latter having shot her four times with a dueling pistol. Almonester survived the shooting, but she apparently still holds a grudge and sometimes takes it out on male employees at Vessel.

Jean Lafitte's Blacksmith Shop Bar

The current building, constructed around 1722, is the oldest structure used as a bar in the United States. It was purported to be the base of operations for Jean Lafitte's contraband business. Long-time bartender Jason Robards can attest to some strange happenings at the bar. He's seen pictures snapped by patrons featuring a thick, misty haze encircling people's heads, occasionally morphing into distinctive shapes—a skull or a man atop a horse, among others—and over the years, patrons have reported seeing full-body apparitions of Lafitte himself.

P. G. T. Beauregard-Keyes House

Among the spirits lingering in this museum on the National Register of Historic Places are its namesake, General Beauregard, and Paul Morphy, the chess champion, who was born in the house in 1837. (His grandfather built the current structure.) The author Frances Parkinson Keyes also owned the house in the 1950s and wrote two of her novels about the former residents. Beauregard inspired *Madame Castel's Lodger*, and Morphy *The Chess Players*. Keyes never actually lived in the main house; she stayed in the old slave quarters in the back because of all the disturbances by the many ghosts. She only used the main house for hosting parties, which must have been some very spirited fêtes.

Pirate's Alley

Adjacent to St. Louis Cathedral, Pirate's Alley was frequented by marauders and privateers during the nineteenth century and used as a market for contraband. Witnesses have reported hearing disembodied voices—speaking in English, French, and Spanish—emanating from the alley, including that of Jean Lafitte bartering for guns from his fellow pirates. The area is also a hangout for numerous ghosts including Père Antoine, a Capuchin priest who was the pastor of the St. Louis church in the late eighteenth century.

VAMPIRE BARS
WITH
KILLER COCKTAILS

Vampire lore and tales of the undead date back centuries. New Orleans is home to some intriguing vampire myths and is the setting for many paranormal entities that are hopefully pure fiction. The vampires and witches made famous by author Anne Rice in her novels are probably the most famous, but you are only scratching the surface with the beasties in those tales.

If you spend enough time in New Orleans you will realize that it's not entirely inconceivable that we have vampires roaming the city. The old cobblestone streets and flickering gas lamps of the buildings dating from the eighteenth and nineteenth centuries create an ideal backdrop to enjoy the bite of a cocktail named Undead Gentleman, The Slayer, or Cajun Bloody Mary.

For the adventurous a visit to one of our numerous so-called vampire bars might just quench your thirst—literally and figuratively. New Orleans's mystical aura, steeped in occult history and cultural heritage, fosters an environment where legends of vampires and myriad paranormal beings and occurrences thrive. It's not difficult to imagine Lestat passing you in Jackson Square or Mary Beth Mayfair strolling through the Garden District.

In this city, whispers of the past linger everywhere if you're attuned to listen. It's not only the spirits themselves, but also the events of yesteryears that have left a palpable impression on every street corner and down every alley.

CAJUN BLOODY MARY

SERVES 2 SOULS

There are countless ways to make a killer Bloody Mary, but we like to make ours with Trinity Vodka. Its infusion of onions, celery, and bell peppers (the New Orleans trinity of ingredients for cooking) perfectly complements the spicy, salty tomato flavor. Bars around town make mini meals out of their Marys by going heavy on the garnishes, so you can leave with your thirst quenched and your belly full for a day of exploring this haunted city!

1 LEMON WEDGE

1 TEASPOON CREOLE SEASONING, PLUS EXTRA TO RIM THE GLASSES

1 QUART TOMATO JUICE, CHILLED

1 CUP ORIGINAL TRINITY VODKA, CHILLED

¼ CUP PREPARED HORSERADISH, DRAINED

JUICE OF 1 LEMON

1 TABLESPOON WORCESTERSHIRE SAUCE

1 OR 2 TEASPOONS TABASCO SAUCE

1 PINCH FINE SEA SALT

1 PINCH CELERY SALT

1 PINCH FRESHLY GROUND BLACK PEPPER

OPTIONAL GARNISHES: PICKLED OKRA, SPICY GREEN BEANS, CELERY STICKS, CARROT STICKS, COCKTAIL OLIVES, LEMON WEDGES, BOILED SHRIMP, BACON, CHERRY TOMATOES, PARSLEY

Rub the lemon wedge around the rims of 2 highball glasses, then roll the rims in Creole seasoning to coat. Fill the glasses with ice cubes.

Fill a large cocktail shaker with cracked ice. Add the Creole seasoning, tomato juice, vodka, horseradish, lemon juice, Worcestershire sauce, Tabasco sauce, sea salt, celery salt, and pepper. Shake vigorously, then strain into the prepared glasses and garnish as desired.

Don't skimp on the garnishes! A proper Bloody Mary should be a meal unto itself. Okra isn't just for your gumbo—it should be pickled and placed in your cocktail along with, for example, spicy green beans, celery sticks, carrot sticks, olives, and lemon wedges. Even proteins like shrimp and bacon are acceptable to add! Just go wild!

BLOOD ORANGE MARGARITA

*This blood-red version of a margarita might just satisfy your lust for blood—
at least for now. If you are searching for some other vamp-worthy cocktails, check out
the Vampire Apothecary where you can choose from frightfully fun dessert cocktails
including a Macabre Martini and After Death, a cognac and Irish Cream concoction
sure to quell the most rabid of cravings. It's a perfect way to end a day of browsing
the nearby Vampyre Boutique for all your undead fashion needs.*

1½ OUNCES BLANCO TEQUILA

¾ OUNCE FRESH RUBY RED GRAPEFRUIT JUICE

½ OUNCE FRESH LIME JUICE

3 OUNCES FRESH BLOOD ORANGE JUICE

½ OUNCE AGAVE NECTAR

1 DASH EL GUAPO FUEGO BITTERS

1 BLOOD ORANGE SLICE, FOR GARNISH

Fill a cocktail shaker with cracked ice. Add the tequila, juices, agave nectar, and bitters. Shake and strain into a lowball glass and garnish with a blood orange slice.

Note: For extra sweetness, rim the glass with granulated sugar before adding ingredients.

LIBATION LAGNIAPPE

To add bite to this recipe, replace the tequila with champagne or vodka.

BLOODY GIN FIZZ

This bloody twist on a classic New Orleans cocktail weaves together vampire legends and the city's history, just like the mysterious tale of Jacques St. Germain. He was believed to be none other than the Comte de St. Germain, an eighteenth-century French count rumored to be a vampire. As the legend goes, St. Germain bit a woman in his French Quarter home. She escaped and alerted the police. When the authorities searched the house, they found no food, only bottles filled with human blood. St. Germain vanished, never to be seen again.

1 EGG WHITE

½ OUNCE FRESH LEMON JUICE

½ OUNCE FRESH LIME JUICE

¾ OUNCE HEAVY CREAM

2 OUNCES GIN

¾ OUNCE SIMPLE SYRUP (PAGE 12)

¾ OUNCE CAJUN OR REGULAR GRENADINE

2 OUNCES CLUB SODA

Place the egg white, juices, cream, gin, and syrup in a cocktail shaker without ice and shake vigorously until the egg white gets frothy, about 15 seconds. Add a few ice cubes and shake again until well chilled. Strain into a highball glass. Add the grenadine and top with the soda water.

THE
SLAYER

There are numerous ways to slay a vampire, but vampires being brought to justice by police? Now that's a new one! In the 1930s, police raided the French Quarter house of the Carter brothers, John and Wayne, both rumored to be vampires. They found four people tied to chairs in the midst of many dead bodies. The captives told the authorities that the brothers collected and drank their blood every evening. Following a trial, the Carters were found guilty and later executed. Some time later, their tomb was opened and found empty.

1 OUNCE VODKA

1 OUNCE TEQUILA

3 OUNCES FRESH LEMON JUICE

3 OUNCES CLUB SODA

1 LIME SLICE. FOR GARNISH

Fill a lowball glass with cracked ice. Add the vodka, tequila, and juice. Slowly add the club soda, then stir to mix. Garnish with the lime slice.

Note: This recipe makes a sour cocktail (because you can't slay a vampire with sweetness)! You can cut back on the lemon juice or, for a sweeter drink, rim the glass with granulated sugar.

VAMPIRE'S KISS

In 1728, a group of young women traveled to New Orleans from France seeking marriage. The women were pale and came with casket-shaped trunks, and their skin immediately reddened and blistered when they emerged into the sunlight. But when nuns went to pack up their belongings, they found the young women had vanished, leaving behind their casket-shaped trunks with unknown contents. Out of fear, the casket trunks were sealed with blessed nails and stored in a convent attic amidst rumors that the women were vampires. This spooky legend of the so-named Casket Girls inspires this creepy and delicious cocktail.

2 OUNCES CRANBERRY BALSAMIC GASTRIQUE (PAGE 12)

2 OUNCES VODKA

2 OUNCES CHAMBORD RASPBERRY LIQUEUR

JUICE OF 1 BLOOD ORANGE

Fill a cocktail shaker with cracked ice. Add the gastrique, vodka, liqueur, and juice. Shake and strain into a chilled martini glass. For extra eeriness, drizzle some of the gastrique down the sides of the glass to resemble blood drips.

LIBATION LAGNIAPPE

A gastrique can raise any cocktail to the next level! For future cocktails, try replacing the cranberries with your favorite berries and the balsamic vinegar with apple cider vinegar.

FANG-RIA

Any red wine sangria tastes spookier when you drink it in a vampire hangout. If you are in New Orleans, make a stop at the Vampire Café. In addition to Fang-ria (their vampire version of sangria), you can also choose one of their "blood type" cocktails, including the universal donor type O negative (a blackberry mojito), or the rarest of blood types, AB negative (basil-infused Bombay gin with grapefruit juice).

1 BOTTLE (750 ML) DRY RED WINE

¾ CUP CRANBERRY JUICE

½ CUP BRANDY

¼ CUP GRANULATED SUGAR

1 MEDIUM, TART APPLE (SUCH AS GRANNY SMITH),
CORED, PEELED, AND SLICED

1 CUP FRESH STRAWBERRIES, SLICED

1 CUP FRESH CRANBERRIES

1 CINNAMON STICK

Combine the wine, juice, brandy, and sugar in a large pitcher and stir until the sugar is fully dissolved. Stir in the apple, strawberries, and cranberries. Drop in the cinnamon stick and refrigerate overnight. Serve in ice-filled glasses of your choice.

JAZZY VAMP

Vampires love nightlife, so what could be better than a jazz club with a super-secret vampire bar hidden within? Proudly holding the title of New Orleans's oldest jazz club in operation, Fritzel's European Jazz Pub is where you can listen to New Orleans-style jazz while sipping a cocktail. And if you're up for a more ethereal experience, you can visit the vampire speakeasy tucked away on the property, accessible only with a special password. The atmosphere in this hidden bar is mystical, and the alcohol-infused potions are first-rate.

½ OUNCE FRESH LEMON JUICE

½ OUNCE EL GUAPO ROSE CORDIAL

1 OUNCE COGNAC

3 OUNCES CHAMPAGNE OR PROSECCO

LEMON PEEL, FOR GARNISH

Fill a cocktail shaker with cracked ice. Add the juice, cordial, and Cognac. Shake well and strain into a champagne flute. Top with the champagne or prosecco and garnish with a lemon peel.

Velvet falernum, a distinctive liqueur blending lime, almond, vanilla, ginger, and clove flavors, is an essential ingredient in Beach's original recipe, with John D. Taylor's being his brand of choice. To make this cocktail more fang-worthy, we swapped it for grenadine. If you fancy a spicier vamp vibe, feel free to substitute allspice dram for the falernum.

UNDEAD GENTLEMAN

This creepy cocktail was invented by New Orleans native Donn Beach, the trailblazer behind the 1930s' tiki movement. Dubbed the Undead Gentleman, the drink graced the menu at his Beachcomber Bar in Hollywood, debuting the day after Prohibition's repeal. It is a variation of the Zombie, Beach's iconic cocktail, and appropriate for the bloodsucking gentlemen (or gentlewomen) of the night. The drink is shaken rather than blended and calls for fewer tiki syrups, making it easier to make at home, ensuring you're never too far away from your coffin or crypt when dawn approaches.

½ TEASPOON ABSINTHE

1½ OUNCES BLENDED AGED RUM

1 OUNCE BLACK BLENDED OVERPROOF RUM

½ OUNCE FRESH WHITE OR PINK GRAPEFRUIT JUICE

½ OUNCE FRESH LIME JUICE

½ OUNCE GRENADINE

½ OUNCE CINNAMON SIMPLE SYRUP (PAGE 12)

1 DASH ANGOSTURA OR PEYCHAUD'S BITTERS

1 LIME SLICE, FOR GARNISH

Place the absinthe in a coupe glass. Swirl it around to coat the interior, then discard any excess absinthe; set the glass aside. Fill a cocktail shaker with cracked or cubed ice. Add the rums, juices, grenadine, syrup, and bitters and shake until well chilled. Double-strain into the prepared glass and garnish with the lime slice.

HAUNTED HISTORY
RAISING THE STAKES

Pat O'Brien's

Original proprietor Pat O'Brien ran a speakeasy in the French Quarter until the end of Prohibition. At the current location, built in 1791, signature Hurricane drinks and amazing Bloody Marys flow freely, as do rumors about the ladies' room and the entire third floor being haunted. Both patrons and staff alike have reported hearing footsteps and seeing the ghost of a restroom attendant, with at least one employee leaving because of all the paranormal activities. The dueling piano bar is also a must-visit and a hot spot for ghosts. People have reported hearing unexplained footsteps, chairs being dragged across the floor, and the tinkling of piano keys when no one was playing.

Fritzel's European Jazz Pub

You didn't hear it from us, but Fritzel's is the location of a speakeasy vampire bar. Potions Lounge has a secret entrance and code needed to enter. Once inside, you can order creepy cocktails, some served in "poison" bottles. We can't tell you all the details, but we'll give you a hint: ask around while you are doing your shopping at Boutique du Vampyre or dining at Vampire Café. If you are deemed worthy, you just might warrant an invitation to spend an evening at this secret lounge. And maybe bring along a stake or two, just in case, to ensure that it's not your last visit!

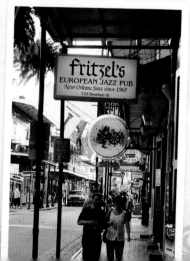

Boutique Du Vampyre and Vampire Apothecary

One of the few true vampire shops in the world, this New Orleans boutique carries such a wide and interesting selection of apparel and accessories—all perfect for the undead. A true one-stop shop for the everyday needs of a vampire, you'll find yourself tempted to purchase some of their "blood," a delightful fruit punch energy drink mixed with vodka and rum.

Nearby is Vampire Apothecary, featuring a full menu complemented by craft cocktails, including Vampyre Vodka Pomegranate Lemonade and Vampire Sazerac, as well as an assortment of vampire-themed coffee and tea blends. They also offer fang-making and psychic services if you are so inclined.

Vampire Café

It is estimated that there are about five thousand people who identify as vampires in the United States. If you are one of them or just interested in vampire culture, plan a visit to Vampire Café, where they are "dying to have you in for a bite." The café features a vampire chef, and you can rest assured that careful precautions have been put in place to protect "nocturnal guests" from contact with silver; only gold utensils are used there. During your visit, you can have a tea leaf reading, tarot card session, or partake in a vampire tour of the city.

Former Residence of Jacques St. Germain, the Vampire Count

Nestled among Royal Street's many antique shops, charming courtyard restaurants, art galleries, and historic museums is the infamous home of Jacques St. Germain, who, if you believe the folklore, was actually the Comte de St. Germain, a centuries-old vampire. The Count first lived in eighteenth-century France and ran in the same circles as King Louis XV and Voltaire, who once said of him, "He is a man who knows everything and who never dies." The Count threw lavish parties but was never seen eating and he never seemed to age. In 1784 he supposedly died but some two hundred years later, another Frenchman, Jacques St. Germain, came to New Orleans. Following a woman's accusation that he bit her neck, a police search of St. Germain's home revealed blood-stained clothing spanning different historical periods and bottles filled with human blood, yet no trace of food. St. Germain fled his Royal Street house and was never seen again, but his legacy and his home live on.

Beachbum Berry's Latitude 29

The irony of New Orleans vamps hanging out in a place with a beach theme is not lost on anyone, but who can blame them? The city is a tiki mecca! Rum cocktails abound on Bourbon Street and throughout French Quarter watering holes, so it should come as no surprise that New Orleans, with its Caribbean influence and love of intricate cocktails, has embraced the tiki movement in the decades following Prohibition. Beachbum Berry's Latitude 29 is an excellent example of the tiki tradition, especially during Spooky Season when it transforms into Beachbum Berry's Haunted Hut. They offer a special spectral cocktail menu that adds the glorious ghoulishness of Halloween to the rum-soaked fever dream of a great tiki joint.

Former Residence of the Carter Brothers

The corner of St. Ann and Royal Streets is where you'll find the former abode of two of the most famous New Orleans vampires. The Carter Brothers lived here in the 1930s and appeared to be normal, hardworking individuals. Nothing seemed amiss until one day, a young girl went into a police station with bandaged wrists and reported to police that she had been abducted and held hostage by the Carters in their home. She recounted being tied to a chair, her wrists deliberately slit—not fatal wounds, but enough for her blood to drain slowly over several days. She also told police that there were others suffering the same fate. Upon investigation, police found four individuals still alive but bound to chairs as well as fourteen dead bodies. The Carters were found guilty of these crimes and executed, their bodies placed in an above-ground tomb as is the custom in New Orleans. Several years later, when the tomb was reopened to bury another body, it was empty. Rumors persist that the brothers are still alive, lurking around their former home; there have been many reports of prowlers matching their exact description.

The Dungeon Bar

Even by New Orleans standards, this is a creepy place. To enter the bar you must pass through a prison cell door at the entrance to an alley marked by a sign that reads, "The Quarter's Most Unique Night Spot." If you can muster up the courage to continue, venture down the alley to the Dungeon Bar. The specialty cocktails here include unique versions of Witches' Brew and Dragon's Blood. Enjoy yourself, but whatever you do, don't take any photos. The vampires hate that, and it's strictly forbidden!

VOODOO & WITCHCRAFT

Voodoo, also spelled Vodou in Haiti and Vodú in Cuba (to spell the religious practice as Voodoo outside of Louisiana is considered offensive), has a long and storied history in the city. New Orleans has its own style of Voodoo, combining elements of Catholicism and Haitian beliefs, fusing spirits, magic, and mystery together. Legendary stories of Voodoo King Dr. John and Marie Laveau, the renowned Creole practitioner, serve as inspirations for concoctions such as Voodoo Juice and The Gris-Gris, while tales of New Orleans witches, both fictional and factual, inspire the New Orleans-style Witches' Brew.

New Orleans Voodoo is rooted in the Vodou religion practiced by enslaved people who fled to the city after the 1791 revolt in Saint-Domingue, leading to the establishment of the Republic of Haiti. In New Orleans Voodoo, the Iwa spirits of Vodou have been replaced by the concept of Catholic saints. The belief is that while the one true God is not involved in the everyday lives and concerns of mortals, the saints can step in to solve problems or offer advice since all mortals need help on occasion.

Witches take the form of Voodoo priestesses in New Orleans. They cast spells and perform rituals commonly attributed to witches. Witchcraft should not automatically be labeled evil since magic can be either black or white, depending on the intent of the practitioner. Likewise, spells can be cast to help people with creativity, careers, fertility, and love just as easily as to revenge or harm them.

On the surface, witchcraft and Voodoo seem to be shrouded in mystery and fear and are often misunderstood, but the traditions and history associated with these practices in New Orleans are rich and deep; their echoes are everywhere if you let yourself listen.

POISON APPLE

Throughout the year, a Voodoo daiquiri from Jean Lafitte's Blacksmith Shop Bar is always a good idea, but when Halloween arrives, their Poison Apple is the most seasonally fitting potion. Inspired by the many versions of Poison Apple cocktails that pop up on seasonal menus across the French Quarter during Spooky Season, this recipe adds a glittery New Orleans twist.

2 OUNCES WHISKEY

1 OUNCE APPLE SCHNAPPS

3 OUNCES CRANBERRY APPLE JUICE

1 DASH EDIBLE GOLD GLITTER

1 CINNAMON STICK, FOR GARNISH
(OPTIONAL)

Fill a cocktail shaker with cracked ice. Add the whiskey, schnapps, juice, and glitter. Shake vigorously and strain into a coupe glass. Garnish with the cinnamon stick , if desired.

LIBATION LAGNIAPPE

Haunts for those interested in witchcraft in New Orleans include Haus of Voodoo, Hex Old World Witchery, and Voodoo Authentica. If you'd prefer to enjoy some witch-themed cocktails, try the seasonally offered Poison Apple at Bar Marilou, a concoction of Calvados apple brandy, baked apples, salted caramel, and cotton candy.

WITCHES' BREW

SERVES 4–6 SOULS

We've all seen stereotypical images of witches: black-cloaked old women with long, crooked noses and unsightly facial warts, usually depicted stirring a cauldron filled with a smoking, unappetizing brew consisting of eye of newt and toe of frog among other oddities not readily available at your local supermarket. Thankfully, this bewitching recipe can be conjured up with much tastier ingredients while still being spellbindingly intoxicating. For added ambience, serve this drink out of a punch bowl or an actual cauldron and place small containers of dry ice around the outside to create the eerie "smoky" effect.

½ CUP CHILLED BLACK VODKA

1 CUP SAZERAC RYE WHISKEY

⅓ CUP FRESH LEMON JUICE

½ CUP APPLE SCHNAPPS

1 QUART (32 OUNCES) CRANBERRY JUICE

Place the vodka, whiskey, lemon juice, schnapps, and cranberry juice in a large pitcher and stir. Immediately serve in punch glasses.

LIBATION LAGNIAPPE

Black vodka gets its coloring from the Asian herb catechu, derived from acacia trees and used as an astringent and dye. Catechu doesn't affect the taste of the vodka, but its dark color provides a different drinking experience. Black vodka, like the delicious one made by UK-based Blavod Drinks, can be difficult to find in the US, so feel free to use any vodka you have on hand.

QUEEN LAVEAU

It's impossible to talk or even think about Voodoo without mentioning Marie Laveau. Known as the Voodoo Queen of New Orleans, she left an indelible mark. Voodoo queens are often associated with evil spells. However, a Voodoo priestess might actually be looked upon fondly by her community and sought out for help with a variety of problems, from health ailments to foretelling the future (and sometimes to change the course of future events). This unusual cocktail, featuring fresh blackberries and elderflower liqueur, is a tonic for the spirit and a tribute to her legacy of healing. Fun fact: Blackberries are native to Louisiana!

3 OUNCES GIN

½ OUNCE SIMPLE SYRUP (PAGE 12)

¼ CUP MUDDLED FRESH BLACKBERRIES

2 OR 3 OUNCES TONIC WATER

1 DASH ST–GERMAIN ELDERFLOWER LIQUEUR

FRESH, WHOLE BLACKBERRIES, FOR GARNISH

Fill a lowball glass halfway with cracked ice. Add the gin and syrup, followed by the blackberries. Top it off with the tonic water and stir. Finish with a dash of St-Germain and garnish with fresh, whole blackberries.

LIBATION LAGNIAPPE

St-Germain is a French-style liqueur made with fresh elderflowers, grown in the Savoie region in France and hand-picked in late spring. With tasting notes of pear, peach, and grapefruit, its flavors are complex yet subtle, making this liqueur both endlessly mixable and delicious to sip on its own.

WITCHY WOMAN

Legends about Voodoo queens in New Orleans are as plentiful as doubloons at Mardi Gras. Among them is Julia Brown (also known as Julia White), an early twentieth-century practitioner who some say still haunts Manchac Swamp after being accused of causing a deadly hurricane that demolished an entire town. The Witchy Woman cocktail packs a powerful punch that rivals Julia's hurricane with the combination of four different spirits.

1½ OUNCES APEROL

1 OUNCE OLD NEW ORLEANS CRYSTAL RUM

1 OUNCE FRESH ORANGE JUICE

½ OUNCE FRESH LIME JUICE

½ OUNCE EL GUAPO CREOLE ORGEAT

1 DASH PEYCHAUD'S BITTERS

1 ORANGE SLICE, FOR GARNISH

1 SPRIG MINT, FOR GARNISH

Fill a lowball glass with cracked ice. Add the Aperol, rum, juices, orgeat, and bitters and stir until well mixed. Garnish with the orange slice and mint sprig.

LIBATION LAGNIAPPE

Orgeat is a cloudy almond-citrus syrup with a pronounced almond flavor that adds a nutty sweetness to cocktails. If you can't find it in stores, you can try your hand at making your own using the recipe on page 13. Amaretto is also a fine substitute in this recipe.

THE
GRIS-GRIS

Whether you want to ward off evil or attract love and success, you will need some help. Gris-gris is a Voodoo talisman or amulet that is believed to protect the wearer from harm or bring good luck. If your needs are not that specific or you just want to cover more ground, you can simply cast a spell or incantation to avoid bad juju (ideally while enjoying this cocktail). Rather than a traditional toast, chant an intent to bring good fortune to all.

¾ OUNCE COGNAC

¾ OUNCE SAZERAC RYE WHISKEY

¾ OUNCE SIMPLE SYRUP (PAGE 12)

¼ OUNCE BÉNÉDICTINE

2 DASHES PEYCHAUD'S BITTERS

1 OR 3 BLACK COCKTAIL CHERRIES, FOR GARNISH

Add the Cognac, whiskey, syrup, Bénédictine, and bitters to a coupe glass and stir. Garnish with the cherries.

LIBATION LAGNIAPPE

Only garnish with an odd number of cherries or you could incur some bad juju.

NIGHT TRIPPER

Although legends surrounding Voodoo often spotlight women, a significant figure in nineteenth-century New Orleans was the Voodoo King, Dr. John. He went by various names like Jean Montanee and Jean Gris-Gris, serving as a Voodoo priest, wizard, and conjurer. The legacy of the original Dr. John was carried on by the New Orleans musician Malcom "Mac" Rebennack, also known as the Night Tripper.

1¾ OUNCES BOURBON

¾ OUNCE AMARO ABANO

¼ OUNCE STREGA

2 DASHES PEYCHAUD'S BITTERS

Fill a cocktail shaker with cracked ice. Add the bourbon, Amaro Abano, Strega, and bitters and shake until well chilled. Strain into a wine glass.

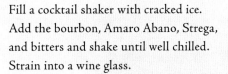

LIBATION LAGNIAPPE

This cocktail was created by Chris Hannah at Jewel of the South in honor of musician Dr. John's reign as king of the Krewe du Vieux Mardi Gras parade in 2010. Chris was watching as Dr. John's float passed by and was inspired to create this drink in the good doctor's honor.

SAINT
75

Marie Leveau and Dr. John may have passed, but Voodoo lives on in New Orleans. In addition to Voodoo, two beloved pastimes are commonly associated with New Orleans—the Saints football team and libations. It is widely believed that the first playoff win for the Saints resulted from a Voodoo ritual performed in the Superdome in 2000. That is cause for a toast!

1 OUNCE GIN

1 OUNCE ST-GERMAIN ELDERFLOWER LIQUEUR

1 OUNCE BASIL SIMPLE SYRUP (PAGE 12)

1 OUNCE FRESH LEMON JUICE

2 OR 3 OUNCES SPARKLING WINE
(SUCH AS CAVA)

1 LEMON PEEL, FOR GARNISH

Fill a cocktail shaker with cracked ice. Add the gin, St-Germain, syrup, juice, and sparkling wine. Shake gently and strain into a chilled champagne flute. Top with the sparkling wine and garnish with the lemon peel.

LIBATION LAGNIAPPE

This cocktail is made with sparkling wine to serve as a pre-game toast filled with anticipation, a post-game celebration for victory, or a pick-me-up after a loss.

In New Orleans, the Krewe of Boo reigns as the official Halloween parade, but there is also a Zombie run through the Warehouse District, the Captain's Masquerade Ball, the Axeman's Ball, the Monster Mash, and a dance-off to help celebrate the season. Additionally, the House of Blues has an annual vampire ball inspired by Anne Rice. There's music, a costume contest, a ritual burlesque, and a Voodoo ritual offering to the vampire spirit queen of New Orleans.

VOODOO JUICE

Voodoo is practiced by some all year long, but it gets special attention around
Halloween. It shouldn't surprise anyone that Spooky Season is big in New Orleans.
In fact, if it wasn't for Mardi Gras, Halloween would be the biggest celebration.
If you haven't experienced Halloween in New Orleans, what are you waiting for?
If this book has conveyed anything, it's that our time here is short, so grab
your Voodoo Juice and laissez les bons temps rouler ("let the good times roll")!

1 OUNCE ORANGE RUM

1 OUNCE PINEAPPLE RUM

1 OUNCE BANANA RUM

1 OUNCE MANGO RUM

1½ OUNCES FRESH ORANGE JUICE

1½ OUNCES PINEAPPLE JUICE

1½ OUNCES APPLE JUICE

½ OUNCE OLD NEW ORLEANS CAJUN SPICE RUM

1 PINEAPPLE WEDGE, FOR GARNISH

Fill a highball glass with cracked ice. Add
the orange, pineapple, banana, and mango
rums and the juices and stir well. Float
the spice rum on top and garnish with the
pineapple wedge.

HAUNTED HISTORY
OCCULT CRASH CORPSE

POPP FOUNTAIN

Built in 1937, this lovely fountain is a popular spot for weddings and other festive gatherings. However, during the 1970s, witches gathered here regularly to perform rituals and cast spells. The Religious Order of Witchcraft, founded by Mary Oneida Toups, was the prominent coven of witches that frequented this place. The coven was recognized as the first acknowledged as a church by the State of Louisiana, and it's still in existence today. Popp Fountain was also referenced in the television series *American Horror Story: Coven*. The mystical quality of this fountain doesn't end with witches; it is also reported to be a time warp. Numerous tales circulate of fountain visitors experiencing the loss of several hours of time while only a few seconds seem to pass.

CONGO SQUARE

Located in Armstrong Park at the convergence of the French Quarter and Tremé, Congo Square holds profound historical significance in the development of jazz, the practice of Voodoo, and the history of enslaved people in New Orleans. The Code Noir, a body of laws enacted in 1724 to control the behaviors of Africans, free people of color, and Native Americans, granted the enslaved Sunday off from their labors. Congo Square emerged in the nineteenth century as the epicenter of their Sunday festivities, where enslaved individuals would sing, dance, and buy and sell goods. The square was also a place where they could express spiritual beliefs and practice Voodoo, with Marie Laveau frequently participating in the rituals there.

Marie Laveau's Tomb

Every day, people flock to Marie Laveau's simple tomb in St. Louis Cemetery No. 1 to bring flowers and other gifts and to perform a Voodoo ritual. They knock three times on the marble slab, draw a cross on it with a piece of soft brick, and place their hand on it asking for the granting of a favor. When alive, Marie held healing ceremonies from her St. Ann Street home, conducting consultations and formulating charms, known as "pwans," to help with relationships, employment, or any other concerns her clients may have had. Legends about Marie are plentiful and difficult to verify; they depict her as a demon, a saint, and everything in between. Marie was illiterate, so she left behind no journals or letters that would give us a glimpse of who she was by her own account. We have only the words of those who knew her and the stories that were passed down.

Holt Cemetery

Unlike the prevalent above-ground cemeteries, Holt Cemetery has below-ground burials. The most famous resident is jazz legend Buddy Bolden. Unlike the standardized commercial headstones and markers seen in the cemeteries of more affluent deceased members of the community, the ones you see at Holt are handcrafted by the deceased's families. The lack of uniformity makes this cemetery very personal and unique. Although Holt is still an active cemetery, its state of disrepair is a serious concern for historians and conservationists, even providing an opportunity for grave robbers. This cemetery is well known among ghost hunters, and it is often the site for various occult rituals.

Manchac Swamp

Swamps are by their very nature spooky and forbidding places, so it's not surprising that stories of unexplained phenomena abound. One story involves the loss of an entire town. In the small town of Frenier, located on the edge of the Manchac Swamp, about twenty-five miles northwest of New Orleans, lived a woman named Julia. Revered as a Voodoo priestess, healer, and oracle, Julia was relied upon by the townsfolk to provide them with healing potions and predict their future. But the people also lived in fear of her, as Julia would often sit on her front porch, singing a prophetic tune of how she would take the whole town with her when she died. And she did just that. When Julia died in September of 1915, the whole town came to her funeral, maybe in fear, out of curiosity, or to appease the spirit of a Voodoo queen. On that same day, a powerful hurricane hit Frenier, destroying it and claiming the lives of all but two residents who were out of town. The survivors buried the 50 souls lost that day in a mass grave. Blamed for the disaster, Julia is said to haunt the swamp to this day.

Voodoo Spiritual Temple

The Voodoo Spiritual Temple is the most famous of the Voodoo temples in New Orleans. It provides everything necessary for the practice of Voodoo, including gris-gris and mojo bags, books, oils and herbs, and jewelry. Beyond supplies, the temple also provides services like consultations, weddings, baptisms, and bone casting, conducted by a Voodoo priest and priestess.

Le Coffre au Trésor

This building currently operates as an antiques shop and is the home of The Haunted Sax. Acquired from an estate sale in Pennsylvania, the saxophone is engraved with the name "Paulette," who may be the presence haunting unsuspecting customers; they report to have seen, felt, and heard her while browsing in the shop. The building also has a history with Voodoo. Back in the 1960s, it housed the shop of the Voodoo Queen Mary Oneida Toups. Known as the Witch Queen, Toups had ties to a famous Voodoo King, Dr. John, through this property. A contemporary of Marie Laveau, Dr. John specialized in fortune-telling and controlling poltergeists. In modern times, the New Orleans musician Malcom "Mac" Rebennack took on the moniker and persona of the original Dr. John in both his music and attire; he was often seen in an elaborate headdress and with a walking stick bedazzled with feathers and beads. His breakout album in the 1960s was even entitled Gris-Gris, and at one time Dr. John lived with The Witch Queen in this building. When the building was up for sale in 2022, one of the selling features listed was a purported magical portal into another space and time.

Superdome

Ava Kay Jones, a Voodoo priestess, was hired by the New Orleans Saints to perform a Voodoo cleansing ceremony in the Superdome on December 20, 2000. The Superdome's parking garage was built over the former Girod Street Cemetery and after thirty-three years without a playoff win, it occurred to New Orleanians that a Voodoo ceremony to remove any curses or bad juju might be in order. Before that day's game, over sixty thousand spectators witnessed Ava's ritual, complete with a boa constrictor around her neck, a Voodoo doll, a gris-gris bag, and a bottle of gin. It worked! The Saints secured their first-ever playoff win by beating the Rams. Some skeptics say that we just got lucky, but Saints fans know better.

SPIRIT GUIDE
HAUNTED NEW ORLEANS MAP

1. Bayou Barataria
   *South-central Jefferson Parish**

2. Beachbum Berry's Latitude 29
   321 North Peters Street

3. Congo Square
   835 North Rampart Street

4. Commander's Palace
   1403 Washington Avenue

5. Former Residence of Jacques St. Germain, the Vampire Count
   1041 Royal Street

6. Former Residence of the Carter Brothers
   800 Block of Royal Street

7. Fritzel's European Jazz Pub
   733 Bourbon Street

8. Greenwood Cemetery
   5200 Canal Boulevard

9. Hotel Monteleone and the Carousel Bar
   214 Royal Street

10. Holt Cemetery
    635 City Park Avenue

11. Hurricane Katrina Memorial and Charity Hospital Cemetery
    5050 Canal Street

12. Jean Lafitte's Blacksmith Shop Bar
    941 Bourbon Street

13. Jewel of the South
    1026 St. Louis Street

14. Josie's Tomb
    Metairie Cemetery
    5100 Pontchartrain Boulevard, Sec. 13

15. Julie's Royal Street House
    734 Royal Street

16. Lafayette Cemetery No. 1
    1400 Washington Avenue

17. LaLaurie House
    1140 Royal Street

18. Le Coffre Au Tresor
    521 St. Philip Street

19. Manchac Swamp
    *St. John the Baptist Parish / Tangipahoa Parish**

20. Marie Laveau's Tomb
    St. Louis Cemetery No. 1, 425 Basin Street

| 21 | May Baily's Place | 31 | St. Louis Cemetery No. 3 |
| 22 | Metairie Cemetery | 32 | St. Roch Cemetery |

21 May Baily's Place
415 Dauphine Street

22 Metairie Cemetery
5100 Pontchartrain Boulevard

23 Muriel's Jackson Square
801 Chartres Street

24 Old Absinthe House and the Belle
Epoque Absinthe Fountain
240 Bourbon Street

25 P. G. T. Beauregard-Keyes House
1113 Chartres Street

26 Pat O'Brien's
718 St. Peter Street

27 Pirate's Alley
Chartres Street at Jackson Square
to Royal Street

28 Popp Fountain
10 Diagonal Drive, City Park

29 Sazerac Bar at the Roosevelt Hotel
130 Roosevelt Way

30 St. Louis Cemetery No. 1
425 Basin Street

31 St. Louis Cemetery No. 3
3421 Esplanade Avenue

32 St. Roch Cemetery
1725 St. Roch Avenue

33 Superdome
1500 Sugar Bowl Drive

34 The Boutique du Vampyre
709 St. Ann Street

35 The Dungeon Bar
738 Toulouse Street

36 The Sultan's Palace
716 Dauphine Street

37 Vampire Apothecary Restaurant and Bar
725 St. Peter Street

38 Vampire Café
801 Royal Street

39 Vessel Restaurant
3835 Iberville Street

40 Voodoo Spiritual Temple
1428 North Rampart Street

*Outside the city, not plotted on map

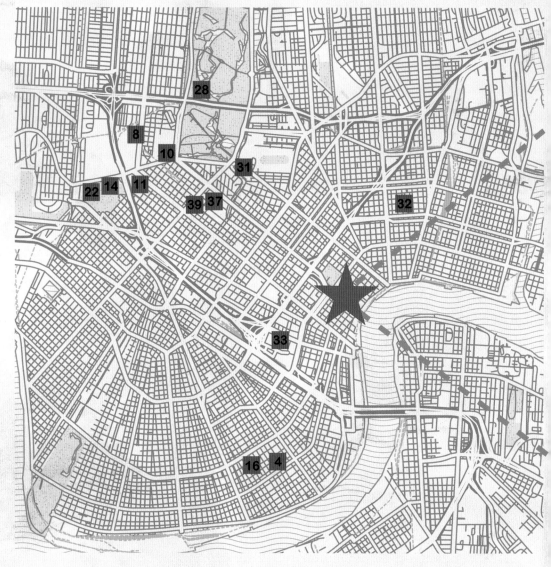

HAUNTINGLY GOOD SPIRITS

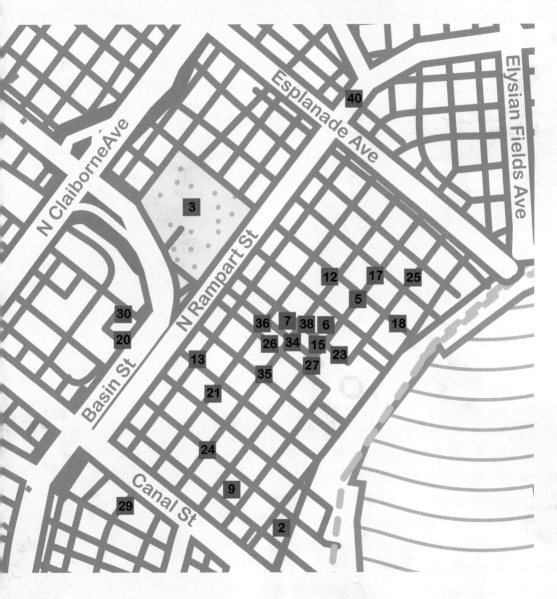

Map labels:
- Elysian Fields Ave
- N Claiborne Ave
- Esplanade Ave
- N Rampart St
- Basin St
- Canal St

Numbered locations:
40, 3, 12, 17, 25, 5, 18, 30, 36, 7, 38, 6, 20, 26, 34, 15, 23, 13, 27, 35, 21, 24, 9, 29, 2

★ *City center detail*

REFERENCES

ARTICLES

Andrew, Scottie. "Inside the world of real-life vampires in New Orleans and Atlanta." CNN. October 29, 2022. https://www.cnn.com/2022/10/29/us/real-vampires-new-orleans-atlanta-cec/index.html

Ann, Jackie. "Few People Know the Story Behind Louisiana's Most Haunted Swamp." Only in Your State. August 20, 2022. https://www.onlyinyourstate.com/louisiana/haunted-swamp-la/

Bell, Michael. "Vampires and Death in New England, 1784 to 1892". Anthropology and Humanism. 31 (2): 124–140. (2006). October 31, 2008. https://anthrosource.onlinelibrary.wiley.com/doi/abs/10.1525/ahu.2006.31.2.124

Browning, John Edgar. "The real vampires of New Orleans and Buffalo: a research note towards comparative ethnography." Palgrave Communications 1, Article number: 15006 (2015). March 24, 2015. https://www.nature.com/articles/palcomms20156

Dash, Toni. "The Grave Digger Cocktail - a Halloween Cocktail with Flavors of Fall." Boulder Locavore. October 24, 2019. https://boulderlocavore.com/the-grave-digger-cocktail/

Difford's Guide for Discerning Drinkers. "Undead Gentleman." January 24, 2023. https://www.diffordsguide.com/cocktails/recipe/16367/undead-gentleman

Encyclopedia.com. "Vodun (Voodoo)." No date. https://www.encyclopedia.com/religion/legal-and-political-magazines/vodun-voodoo

Ferguson, Colleen. "Deadly Cocktails and Their History." Seven Ponds. June 4, 2019. https://blog.sevenponds.com/cultural-perspectives/deadly-cocktails/

Hidden Libations Staff. "The Dungeon: New Orleans Secret Vampire Bar." Hidden Libations. November 5, 2018. https://www.hiddenlibations.com/new-orleans-secret-vampire-bar-the-dungeon/

LeCompte, Lillian. "Vampires in the Deep South: The Casket Girls and Comte de St. Germain." Terrebonne Parish Library System. September 29, 2022. https://mytpl.org/project/vampires-in-the-deep-south-the-casket-girls-and-comte-de-st-germain/

Liquor.com. "Death in the Afternoon." January 7, 2021. https://www.liquor.com/recipes/death-in-the-afternoon/

Maccash, Doug. "This $1.2M French Quarter property might include a magic portal to another spiritual plane." Nola.com. June 15, 2021. https://www.nola.com/news/business/this-1-2m-french-quarter-property-might-include-a-magic-portal-to-another-spiritual-plane/article_593cba6a-ec47-11ec-962c-3b4b7afcc79a.html

Middleton, Ryn. "Jacques St. Germain, The Infamous Louisiana Vampire." Pelican State of Mind. October 30, 2018. https://pelicanstateofmind.com/louisiana-love/jacques-st-germain/

Mix That Drink. "Undertaker Cocktail Recipe, with espresso, Kahlua, vanilla vodka." December 28, 2023. https://mixthatdrink.com/undertaker/

New Orleans & Company. "History of Voodoo in New Orleans." No date. https://www.neworleans.com/things-to-do/multicultural/traditions/voodoo/

New Orleans Restaurants. "Best Bloody Marys in New Orleans." No date. https://www.neworleansrestaurants.com/guides/bloody-marys-new-orleans

O'Neil, Darcy. "Wet Grave." Art of Drink. October 30, 2010. https://www.artofdrink.com/cocktail/the-wet-grave/

Olsen, Whitney Jones. "Vampirism." Encyclopedia.com. No date. https://www.encyclopedia.com/social-sciences/encyclopedias-almanacs-transcripts-and-maps/vampirism

Overhiser, Sonja. "Death in the Afternoon Cocktail." A Couple Cooks. November 28, 2020. https://www.acouplecooks.com/death-in-the-afternoon-cocktail/

Santana, Rebecca. "Hurricane Ida dislodged caskets 'like they were cardboard boxes'; some still scattered." Nola.com. October 21, 2021. https://www.nola.com/news/hurricane/hurricane-ida-dislodged-caskets-like-they-were-cardboard-boxes-some-still-scattered/article_872a42b4-2b89-11ec-96d6-eb8608f30f58.html

Tipsy Bartender. "The Graveyard." January 17, 2018. https://tipsybartender.com/recipe/the-graveyard

Triplett, Mike. "That time the Saints used a Voodoo priestess to end Superdome curse." ESPN. December 16, 2019. https://www.espn.com/nfl/story/_/id/28283702/that-saints-used-voodoo-priestess-end-superdome-curse

VAMzzz Occult Blog. "Doctor John (Jean Montenee, Jean Montanet) – the original New Orleans Voodoo King." March 3, 2021. https://vamzzz.com/blog/doctor-john-or-jean-montenee-new-orleans-voodoo-king/

Wang, Yanan. "Inside the human blood-drinking, 'real vampire' community of New Orleans." *The Washington Post*. October 26, 2015. https://www.washingtonpost.com/news/morning-mix/wp/2015/10/26/inside-the-human-blood-drinking-real-vampire-community-of-new-orleans/

Wexelman, Alex. "A Literary City Guide to New Orleans." The Culture Trip. July 13, 2023. https://theculturetrip.com/northamerica/usa/louisiana/new-orleans/articles/the-culture-trip-literary-city-guide-to-new-orleans

Wilkinson, Nate. "The Undead Gentleman (Smuggler's Cove Recipe)." The Jolly Bartender. June 14, 2017. https://www.jollybartender.com/2017/06/the-undead-gentleman-smugglers-cove.html

Yesterday's America Editorial Team. "The Forgotten History of Two New Orleans Vampires." Yesterday's America. May 19, 2020. https://yesterdaysamerica.com/the-forgotten-history-of-two-new-orleans-vampires/

BOOKS & MAGAZINES

Duggal, Barbara Rosendale. "Marie Laveau: The Voodoo Queen Repossessed." In Creole: *The History and Legacy of Louisiana's Free People of Color*, edited by Sybil Kein, 157-178. Baton Rouge, LA: LSU Press, 2000.

Holland, Eileen. *The Wicca Handbook*. York Beach, ME: Weiser Books, 2000.

Klein, Victor C. *New Orleans Ghosts*. Chapel Hill, N.C.: Professional Press, 1993.

Morrow Long, Carolyn. *A New Orleans Voudou Priestess: The Legend and Reality of Marie Laveau*. Gainesville, FL: University Press of Florida, 2006.

Nott, G. William. "Marie Laveau, Long High Priestess of Voudouism in New Orlean." *New Orleans Times-Picayune*. November 19, 1922. Sunday Magazine, 2.

Rose, Al. Storyville, *New Orleans*. Birmingham, AL: University of Alabama Press, 1997.

Smith, Katherine. *Ghosts and Vampires of New Orleans*. New Orleans, LA: De Simonin Publications, 1998.

INTERVIEWS

Chris Hannah (mixologist), interview by Sharon Keating and Christi Keating Sumich, Jewel of the South, New Orleans, LA, July 11, 2023 and December 7, 2023.

Julie Hollings (senior account executive) interview by Sharon Keating and Christi Keating Sumich, Palm & Pine, New Orleans, LA, July 10, 2023.

Amandalyn Picolo (executive chef and general manager) interview by Sharon Keating and Christi Keating Sumich, Vessel, New Orleans, LA, July 19, 2023.

Jason Robards (bartender), interview by Sharon Keating and Christi Keating Sumich, Lafitte's Blacksmith Shop Bar, New Orleans, LA, May 4, 2023.

OTHER SOURCE MATERIAL

Plessy v. Ferguson, 163 U.S. 537, 538, 16 S. Ct. 1138, 1138, 41 L. Ed. 256 (1896), overruled by Brown v. Bd. of Ed. of Topeka, Shawnee Cnty., Kan., 347 U.S. 483, 74 S. Ct. 686, 98 L. Ed. 873 (1954).

Southern Food and Beverage Museum
1504 Oretha Castle Haley Boulevard, New Orleans, LA
southerfood.org

WEBSITES

Ace Hotel New Orleans. https://acehotel.com/new-orleans/.

Bar Marilou. https://www.barmarilou.com/.

Commander's Palace. https://www.commanderspalace.com/.

Jewel of the South. https://www.jewelnola.com/.

Krewe of Boo. https://www.kreweofboo.com/.

Lafitte's Blacksmith Shop Bar. http://www.lafittesblacksmithshop.com/Homepage.html.

Palm & Pine. https://www.palmandpinenola.com/.

The Roots of Music. https://therootsofmusic.org/.

Voodoo Spiritual Temple. https://voodoospiritualtemple.org/.

PHOTOGRAPHY CREDITS

Cover Adobe Stock/eugenegg. **Page 5** Adobe Stock/Victoria Avvacumova. **Page 18** Shutterstock/ Suzanne C. Grim. **Page 21** Shutterstock/Brent Hofacker. **Page 22** Shutterstock/Gleti. **Page 25** Shutterstock/enjoysun24. **Page 26** Shutterstock/Brent Hofacker. **Page 29** Shuttertock/Derek Tedders. **Page 30** ShutterstockAuster Pics. **Page 33** Adobe Stock/Julia. **Page 34** Shutterstock/ Maria Shipakina. **Page 36** ShutterstockAtomazul (left), Shutterstock/Nick Tropiano (right). **Page 37** Shutterstock/James Kirkiki,(left), Shutterstock/Anna Westman (right). **Page 38** Tim Graham / Alamy Stock Photo, William Morgan/Alamy Stock Photo. **Page 39** Shutterstock/ Wirestock Creators, Beth Dixson/ Alamy Stock Photo. **Page 40** Everyday Artistry Photography/ Alamy Stock Photo. **Page 43** Shutterstock/pausestudio. **Page 44** Shutterstock/ Mateusz Gzik. **Page 47** Shutterstock/ edpo. **Page 47** Shutterstock/Brent Hofacker. **Page 51** Shutterstock/ Maksym Fesenko. **Page 52** Shutterstock/Dimitriy_Kul. **Page 55** Shuttrestock/Only 4K Ultra HD. **Page 56** Shutterstock/Elena Gordeichik. **Page 58,** Shuterstock/Scott A . Burns, Richard Cummins/Alamy Stock Photo. **Page 59** Jim West/Alamy Stock Photo, Jim West /Alamy Stock Photo. **Page 60** Andre Jenny/Alamy Stock Photo, Wiskerke/Alamy Stock Photo, Shutterstock/ William A. Morgan. **Page 61** Beth Dixson/Alamy Stock Photo, The History Collection/Alamy Stock Photo. **Page 62** Shutterstock/travelview. **Page 65** Shutterstock/HandmadePictures. **Page 66** Shutterstock/Iryna Tsiareshka. **Page 68** Adobe Stock/murziknata. **Page 70** Shutterstock/ Bochkarev Photography. **Page 73** Shutterstock/ Micaela Fiorellini. **Page 74** Shutterstock/Andrei Mayatnik. **Page 77** Shutterstock/Aleksei Isachenko. **Page 78** Shutterstock/Wirestock Creators. **Page 80** Shutterstock/DMBrooks (left), Wayne Keating (right). **Page 81** Wayne Keating (left), Shutterstock/Wangkun Jia(center), Shutterstock/Elliott Cowand Jr(right). **Page 82** Wayne Keating. **Page 83** Stephen Saks Photography/Alamy Stock Photo (left), Shutterstock/jejim (center), Shutterstock/RaksyBH (right). **Page 85** Adobe Stock/Natalia Bratslavsky. **Page 87** Adobe Stock/ Brent Hofacker. **Page 88** Shutterstock/Brent Hofacker. **Page 91** Shutterstock/Brent Hofacker. **Page 92** Adobe Stock/catsanddrinks. **Page 95** Shutterstock/Mariyana M. **Page 96** The Picture Pantry/ Alamy Stock Photo. **Page 99** Shutterstock/VDB Photos. **Page 100** Shutterstock/ Nicole Kandi. **Page 102** Wayne Keating (right), Shuttesrtock/James Kirkikis(right). **Page 103** Wayne Keating. **Page 104** Wayne Keating, **Page 105** The Historic New Orleans Collection, Acc. No. 1986.125.30. (left). Wayne Keating (right). **Page 106** shutterstock/jgale. **Page 109** Shutterstock/etaruscas. **Page 110** Shutterstock/J_K. **Page 113** Shutterstock/Tasha Kendall. **Page 114** Adobe Stock/ vxnaghiyev. **Page 117** Adobe Stock/Mykola Khalavka. **Page 118** Shutterstock/Georgy Malevich. **Page 121** Shutterstock/Dorota Saran. **Page 122** Shutterstock/Alexander Prokopenko. **Page 124** Shutterstock/KJones 504 (left), Shutterstock/William A. Morgan. **Page 125** Irene Abdou/Alamy Stock Photo (left), Serhii Chrucky/Alamy Stock Photo. **Page 126** Shutterstock/Pattie Steib (left), Irene Abdou/Alamy Stock Photo (right) **Page 127** Wayne Keating (left) Carmen K. Sisson/ Cloudybright/Alamy Stock Photo (right). **Page 143** Wayne Keating

135

BOOZE WITH BOOS

COCKTAIL INDEX BY MAIN SPIRIT

INDEX

HAUNTINGLY GOOD SPIRITS

ACKNOWLEDGMENTS

This book would not have been possible without the help of many souls.

A heartfelt thank you to everyone on the Quarto team for making this book come to life! Special thanks to Rage Kindelsperger for seeing the potential in our book, the marketing team for their expertise, and to the ever-patient Cara Donaldson for her support and suggestions.

Thanks to Wayne "Fatwayne" Keating for letting us drag him all over town with his trusty camera.

We are grateful to everyone who shared recipes with us, especially Chris Hannah at Jewel of the South, Kimberly Patton-Bragg at Palm & Pine, Roulaison Distillery, and the folks at Vessel.

Thanks to Jason Robards for taking time to relay the haunted happenings at Lafitte's Blacksmith Shop with us.

None of this would have been possible without our families who supported us by mixing and taste-testing the cocktails. Y'all are always ready to help when we need you!

And, finally, we must acknowledge that without the unique vibe and history of the City of New Orleans, the most interesting and most haunted city in America, there would be no book.

ABOUT THE AUTHORS

A life-long New Orleanian, **SHARON KEATING** is a lawyer by profession. She is also a student of the colorful history, unique customs, and varied architecture of New Orleans. She has served as a licensed tour guide for the City of New Orleans and has volunteered for several tourist information organizations. Sharon is the author of *New Orleans in Photographs*, and *New Orleans Then and Now*, and was a contributor to the website New Orleans for Visitors. Sharon has had many years of experience hosting numerous galas and fundraisers in her 150-year-old haunted home, along with Cornelia, the party-loving ghost. She is very familiar with both liquid and otherworldly spirits.

CHRISTI KEATING SUMICH holds a PhD in history from Tulane University and also holds a Master's degree in English. She is a lifelong resident of New Orleans, Louisiana, and has taught history classes at Tulane University and Loyola University New Orleans. Christi is the author of *Divine Doctors and Dreadful Distempers*. Her research interests include the social history of death and disease. She is Halloween obsessed and a fan of all things spooky season, including her black cat, Admiral Randall Fancypants.

Sharon and Christi are co-authors of *The Brandy Milk Punch*. Together this mother-daughter duo has been mixing up libations using local ingredients since Christi was tall enough to reach the bar.

Library of Congress Control Number:
2023952245

First published in 2024 by Wellfleet Press,
an imprint of The Quarto Group,
142 West 36th Street, 4th Floor,
New York, NY 10018, USA
(212) 779-4972 www.Quarto.com

Group Publisher: Rage Kindelsperger
Editorial Director: Erin Canning
Creative Director: Laura Drew
Managing Editor: Cara Donaldson
Editorial Assistants: Krista Orejudos and
Tobiah Agurkis
Cover and Interior Design: Tara Long

Printed in China

HAUNTINGLY GOOD SPIRITS is intended
only for responsible adults of legal drinking age
in the United States of America (21 years old or
older). Please do NOT drink and drive. If you
need transportation, use a designated driver or a
taxi service. And please be careful when crossing
the street after drinking.

HAUNTINGLY GOOD SPIRITS does
not advocate or encourage the abuse of
alcoholic beverages. Please drink responsibly
and in moderation. We do not, under any
circumstances, accept responsibility for any
damages that result to yourself or anyone else
due to the consumption of alcoholic beverages
or the use of this book and any materials located
in it. We cannot take any responsibility for the
effect these drinks may have on people. As such,
we do not accept liability for any loss, damage, or
inconvenience that occurs as a result of the use
of this book or your reliance upon its content.

Wellfleet titles are also available at discount
for retail, wholesale, promotional, and bulk
purchase. For details, contact the Special Sales
Manager by email at specialsales@quarto.com
or by mail at The Quarto Group, Attn: Special
Sales Manager, 100 Cummings Center Suite
265D, Beverly, MA 01915 USA.

10 9 8 7 6 5 4 3 2 1

ISBN: 978-1-57715-429-7

Digital edition published in 2024
eISBN: 978-0-7603-8887-7